NLP 2.0 Mastery
How to Analyze People

Discover How to Read and Influence People with Proven Body Language and Persuasion Methods, Even if You are a Clueless Beginner

By John Clark

© Copyright 2018 - All rights reserved.

The following book is reproduced below with the goal of providing information that is as accurate and reliable as possible. Regardless, purchasing this book can be seen as consent to the fact that both the publisher and the author of this book are in no way experts on the topics discussed within and that any recommendations or suggestions that are made herein are for entertainment purposes only. Professionals should be consulted as needed prior to undertaking any of the action endorsed herein.

This declaration is deemed fair and valid by both the American Bar Association and the Committee of Publishers Association and is legally binding throughout the United States.

Furthermore, the transmission, duplication, or reproduction of any of the following work including specific information will be considered an illegal act irrespective of if it is done electronically or in print. This extends to creating a secondary or tertiary copy of the work or a recorded copy and is only allowed with the express written consent from the Publisher. All additional right reserved.

The information in the following pages is broadly considered a truthful and accurate account of facts and as such, any inattention, use, or misuse of the information in question by the reader will render any resulting actions solely under their purview. There are no scenarios in which the publisher or the original author of this work can be in any fashion deemed liable for any hardship or damages that may befall them after undertaking information described herein.

Additionally, the information in the following pages is intended only for informational purposes and should thus be thought of as universal. As befitting its nature, it is presented without assurance regarding its prolonged validity or interim quality. Trademarks that are mentioned are done without written consent and can in no way be considered an endorsement from the trademark holder.

Congratulations on downloading *NLP: The Ultimate Guide to Manipulation* and thank you for doing so.

This book is meant to be an introduction and guide to NLP or Neuro-Linguistic Programming. Basically, NLP is the science and art of excellence, which was created from looking at how the top people in various careers were able to obtain their results. The communication skills herein can be learned by everyone to help their effectiveness both professionally and personally

Thanks again for choosing this book! Every effort was made to ensure it is full of as much useful information as possible. Please enjoy!

Table of Contents

Introduction 5
Introduction to NLP 6
    The Subconscious Mind 14
    Secret Driving Habits 18
Development and Learning... 24
    Perspective... 30
Take Charge of Your Mind 34
    Your Inner Voice.. 41
    Dropping Anchors 43
    Dissociation 46
    Content Reframing 48
The Art of Persuasion and Manipulation 49
    Habitual Thinking 51
    Meta-Programs of NLP 52
    Internal Representation 55
    Communication Model... 58
    Three Components of NLP 62
Analyzing Body Language and the Mind 63
    Understanding Body Language................................. 64
    Meta Model.. 68
    The Right Questions 72
    Personal Beliefs 76
Building Connections 79
    Building Rapport 80
    Using Your Words and Voice 87
    Conflict Resolution 91
NLP Applications 96
Conclusion 98

Introduction

You will find many NLP models that will help you in every aspect of your life and career. The approach you will find is practical, you will see results and it is growing in influence in many different disciplines.

Since NLP is constantly growing and evolving and this book is static, it will work as a snapshot of NLP. Even though things may be different tomorrow, it doesn't mean that the practice in this book won't be helpful.

You should view this information as a stepping stone. It is giving you a chance to explore a new area and to keep your life exciting. This book is meant for the beginner to easily understand what to do without confusion.

NLP is a state of mind and a way of being. NLP is something practical that has to be done. While reading about it will teach you a lot, you have to actively practice it to reap any benefits. You will find sets of models, techniques, and skills that will change the way you act and think. This is meant to be useful and to improve your life.

You have to find out what works by doing it. Then you can figure out what didn't work and then work with that until you are able to make it work. This is the great thing about NLP. Let's get started.

There are plenty of books on this subject on the market, so thanks again for choosing this one! Every effort was made to ensure it is full of as much useful information as possible. Please enjoy!

Introduction to NLP

A person's behavior is based on specific structures. With NLP or Neuro-Linguistic Programming, the way that people act, speak, and think is examine with models. Richard Bandler has patterned these models. In the beginning, he patterned his work after characters like Virginia Stair, Fritz Perls, and Milton Erickson, who were seen to have amazing behavioral and linguistic abilities.

Your own experiences are the main uses of the NLP system. There is no way to learn NLP through sequential steps and techniques. However, programmers become skilled at using methods to change how the brain functions and perceives. Its goal is to create a good foundation of attitude and skill so that they can produce new techniques and approaches to self-preserve.

You aren't going to only depend on steps and techniques that are taught to you. You are going to learn how to create new steps so that you can continually achieve success. It works as an investigation of knowledge that will use different stage of human attitude and development, as well as thought formation.

It is going to give you effective tools and strategies that will define who you are, the role you play, and your ideal state of success. While the initial state begins with you, the process will involve all of those around you and the environment to create the best mindset.

The purpose behind NLP is to work as a toolbox of thoughts, skills, and attitudes. The models will become patterns through which your habits will change and be redefined. When you plan on using NLP, you are aiming for personal development and success.

NLP can also make you successful. Whether you are faced with problems in your family, work, or leisure, NLP will give you the ability to alter your outlook and view towards the world. You will start to notice the important meaning of life and what priorities are important in your life. Once you are able to find your strong and weak areas, you will be able to focus on what will make you successful and efficient.

NLP will also improve communication. Positive thinking is able to be changed into words. You will end up becoming more verbally competent when you learn how to change your thoughts and emotions and the way you share perspectives and how you communicate with others. Communication is an amazing method that will give you a better influence, a larger network of friends, and a better way to express yourself.

NLP will also bring together the mind, body, and emotions. There are a lot of people who experience difficulty putting all of the plans into actionable steps. Other people aren't able to learn from their experiences. When these things happen, it means that your mind, body, and emotions aren't working together. Through the use of NLP, you will be able to make connections with each aspect of your existence. NLP will allow all of these aspects to work together so that you can reach success.

To help explain NLP, let's take a look at the history. NLP was first created in the '70s by Richard Bandler and John Grinder. This development was created at the University of California and supervised by Gregory Bateson. Bandler, Bateson, and Grinder were influenced by Alfred Korzybski because of his theories surrounding human presuppositions and modeling.

Other contributors to the theory were Leslie Cameron-Bandler, David Gordon, Judith DeLozier, and Robert Dilts.

Grinder and Bandler worked on the NLP theory until they had a falling out in the '80s. Ginder and DeLozier later created the New Code which took a mind and body approach. Bandler's approach looked at Ericksonian submodalities and hypnosis. Michael Hall mainly looked at mental states and neuro-semantics.

Ted James looked at the best periods of life for therapy and Anthony Robbins made use of products that use NLP. At this point, NLP had been managed and created in different independent sectors. It had also grown and been renamed several times over. Then again, it has also suffered from a lack of definition and regulation.

After many different legal battles, legally, NLP has now become a generic term. Even after all of these years, NLP practitioners still don't have an agreement in regard to the theory. That's why a lot of people have abused it. Still, a lot of the work is dependent on the ideas of the co-developers and other such individuals. For a person to formally practice NLP for human development and condition, they will need to become certified.

Why is it called Neuro-Linguistic Programming? "Neuro" refers to the brain, which what controls your behavior and actions and it stores your memories and experiences. "Linguistic" comes from the word language. This means the "neuro-linguistic" refers to how language affects the brain. Non-verbal cues, words, and symbols are able to cause a response. "Programming" is used to describe the mechanism that is analogous to a computer program.

There are presuppositions of Neuro-Linguistic Programming. The NLP foundation comes with a few basic presuppositions.

Every technique, model, and strategy that is connected to NLP is used along with these assumptions. Since NLP studies the subjective experience, an assumption would be that people can determine objective reality.

The perfect or best direction for life is non-existent. This is the reason why a person can only reach the best possible moment and hope that they have the correct attitude to make the best choices. A person's objective in using NLP is to find excellence and wisdom. Once you widen your choices, you will also be improving your odds of finding excellence. When you are able to acquire different views of the environment, you will gain wisdom.

A territory and a map are not the same things. You can't live your life with only one direct route. Humans are given several different options on the ways that they can live their lives. Depending on what your experiences and perceptions are, you will make decisions that you take you on different paths.

You are in possession of a map to your reality, which will involve a representation of you and those around you. With this map, you will be able to react to the world and be able to better understand yourself. However, if you end up having too much discrepancy between your personal map and territory, you could end up getting lost.

Your life and mind work in systematic processes. There is always going to be an interaction between two people or between a person and the environment. Everything within the universe is connected to each other. When something in your mind or life is affected, your whole experience will absorb what happens. This connection is needed to keep a constant balance.

Communication elicits a response and it comes with a meaning. The manner and content of the reply you receive from the person you are communicating with is the point of your communication. Even if you are aiming to deliver a certain message, validation of understanding can only happen when one person has responded properly.

For example, if you are telling a joke and the person you were telling it to didn't laugh or understand it, then the manner of your telling of the joke didn't help your expected response.

There are two levels of communication — conscious and unconscious. Verbal communication is only one form of communication. A lot of people aren't aware of the fact that they use a lot of body language, facial expressions, posturing, hand and eye movements, and non-verbal cues while they are talking. People are even able to add to the tone and mood of the conversation to relay the message more effectively. Take the statement, "Get out of here." This statement can be communicated in several different ways that could relay a positive or negative message.

Communication can't fail, it only gets an outcome. A person can't say that their communication was useless or was a failure if they didn't get the response they wanted. All it means is that the result ended up being different than what they had expected. This should influence the person to enhance their skills and attitude in regards to communication. You must learn from unpleasant outcomes so that you can identify and gauge the things that kept you from sending out the correct message.

Rapport, which we talk in depth about later on, relates to people according to their world. Each person is able to make their own model or representation of the world that are based on their understanding of environmental influences and previous experiences. This is the reason why you will need to exert some effort if you want to create a new model.

It's important that you are able to see the world as others do so that you can build rapport and communicate effectively. If you keep your mind close in regards to their representation, you will likely have a very hard time getting the response you are looking for. Other people could have a hard time understanding your model.

If a communicator is inflexible, it will be seen through their resistance. When you find that the person you are talking with is resistant, this doesn't mean that they are closed off to the communication. It could mean that you have established rapport. Thus, you will need to enter into their world model. Otherwise, they won't be able to unconsciously receive your message. You also need to learn how you can become flexible so that you are able to understand and speak their language. This is especially true because they can't understand yours. You could end up insulting them without knowing it if you aren't flexible.

You don't have to obtain new things just so that you can be a good leader or communicator. You don't have to obtain new things to create positive changes. You have everything that you already need. All of the mental, emotional, and behavioral resources are within you.

If you aren't able to see them, then you haven't created an access to them. You are not aware of your strengths. You could have a lot of chronic stressors that will keep you from using them. Through NLP, you will be able to be more aware of the resources you have and learn how to correctly use them.

Your positive worth will stay the same even if your internal and external behavior is in question. All humans have worth and dignity no matter what their thoughts and actions are. Then there are good and bad behaviors that will determine their judgment of worth to themselves and the environment.

Your value won't change no matter how bad you act. The value of your actions and behavior are measured based on the expectations of those around you. You are able to change your bad actions and manners so that you can come into alignment with your values.

Every behavior is meant to have a good outcome. However, not every behavior is supposed to be done with positive manners. There are self-preserving mechanisms that are meant for personal benefits. The process of this goal can be dangerous for you and others. These types of behaviors could be unconscious. Your mind and body have a tendency to think about a positive outcome and end up neglecting negative manners.

You have to make sure that you don't rush into decisions or actions without getting the information that you need. You also need to make sure that you take the time to calm down. Disrupted emotions and haste will often cause inadequacy in your actions and bad judgment. You have to be able to differentiate automated and conscious responses. You also need to be able to see the difference between ideals and realities. You should give yourself a reality check every now and again so that you can up your odds of making the best decision.

The process of NLP assimilates subjective experiences. Ever since the moment you started to remember your life events, your brain has worked tirelessly to store information. This information is then recalled through memories and experiences that are changed into personal beliefs and perceptions. These beliefs could be negative or positive depending on how you react to your previous experiences. Positive beliefs can be kept and negative ones can be replaced by positive ones.

NLP works by changing your false or negative understandings. When you are able to connect your brain to your senses, you will find that you can let go of negative feelings, vague thoughts, and traumatic experiences. You have the power to get rid of whatever is hindering you from living a successful and happy life.

For NLP to be effective, every part needs to work together. The first part is the neurological aspect. Your nervous system will take in your experiences using the five senses — smell, taste, touch, hearing, and sight. Your nervous system will then send out signals to the brain so that you can make sense of them.

Then you have the language aspect. This includes verbal and non-verbal communication. These systems of communication order and code your neural representations to provide them meaning. The last part is programming. This is your brain's ability to organize the information from each system. The organization is the way that you achieve specific results and goals. When all three systems are used in unison, you will get a synergistic effect. This allows you to get your desired results.

NLP will help you to perform several different functions. As I have said, it will help your communication skills. NLP can be used to create behavioral changes in others and ourselves. It will provide you with different perspectives of the outside world. These new perspectives will help you to adjust your behaviors and attitudes.

Through NLP, you will become more aware of the things you do. Most people don't pay attention to their actions and thoughts. NLP provides you with a process that will keep you grounded and in control.

Everybody sees the world through different filters. These filters will use different beliefs and values. NLP can help you get rid of these filters. This will give you a better view of the other person's point of view. It will also give you the ability to understand how your actions will affect the lives of others.

NLP is able to create a real difference. You will find improved information. You are able to use this improved information to make the best decisions. The better decisions will bring you better actions. Better actions will give you better results.

The Subconscious Mind

Do you remember the song, "Should I Stay or Should I Go?" This is a great example of something that everything will experience from time to time. It's that inner conflict that makes it feel like one part of us want to do one thing, and then another part is interested in doing something else. Or it could manifest when we feel uncertain about what we actually want to do.

Trying to create change in yourself is easy when everything is congruent, meaning that you are in harmony with yourself and completely dedicated to making the change. You end up being incongruent when you go through an internal conflict which doesn't facilitate your change process. Internal conflict will come up when you split yourself between wanting to do two different things at one time but you can't do both at the same time. For example, when somebody asks you to do a favor, you are torn between wanting to help them and continue doing what you are currently doing. This is when your tone of voice and body language changes. You may tell them — yes, but your body signs won't show the same enthusiasm.

Another example would be when you feel uncertain between two conflicting choices. A part of you is going to want to do something while the other part has a different idea. At that moment, you want to do both of those things.

Incongruence can also be noticed in pleasant conflicts such as part of you wants to go to the beach and another part wants to go to the mountains. The important thing is when incongruence causes a conflict with your values. Let's take this as an example, your boss told you that you need to show a certain customer more aggression. To you, being aggressive means that you are being pushy and pushiness goes against your values.

There will be times when you find yourself associated with incongruent people who will cause you to feel unsure of yourself as to the best way to handle them. They could agree to go along with you or do something, but their face tells you a different story. Other types of incongruent people will tell you that they will do something for you, but they end up changing their mind.

You have probably had times where you didn't have a doubt in your mind and everything was going smoothly. A lot of people call this as "being in the zone." This is how you know you are congruent. Figuring out when you are and when you aren't congruent is a very good life skill. The more aware you are of your own signals of incongruence, the quicker you will be at resolving the conflict. The faster you are able to resolve your incongruence, the easier things will become since you won't be spinning your wheels and unconsciously debating or resisting something.

Incongruence causes a lot of friction in your life. It will take a lot of energy to overcome that part of you that wants to do something that opposes a course of action. The more you work at overriding that part, the more likely it will become that the other part of you is going to object. And when you are faced with fighting with yourself, you normally always lose.

It's a lot easier and more effective to develop the ability to notice when you are incongruent and fix it. It is one of the easier skills to develop and it gives you the most reward. The biggest source of physical and emotional stress is when your mind is trying extremely hard to override the big desire of your body to keep you from doing something that will violate your values. The best way to live a fulfilling life is to move in harmony with your values.

- Recognizing Incongruence

You have probably had several recent moments of being congruent about something. Take a moment to think of the first one of those recent moments that you can think of. Now, take a moment to very specifically remember the place and time where you had that feeling. Remember what you felt, what you heard, and what and who you saw. Remember that moment as if you were living right now. What is it that you are seeing? What things are you hearing? What do you feel?

Recalling that moment is pretty empowering, right? Now pick an aspect of that moment, whether it is a picture, something you felt, or something you heard. The aspect needs to be what is most important to you. This is all in your mind, so whichever element seems the most important to you at that moment.

Now, place that to the side and think about the opposite. Think of a moment when you were uncertain. A moment where you felt extremely ambivalent about something that you needed to do. You will likely find that it's easier to come up with an example when you think about the last time a person asked you to do something and you didn't want to.

Take that feeling, image, or sound you have and magnify it. Make it grow larger, louder, stronger, or brighter. You want to make sure that you are able to recognize it each time it happens. This will be your warning. This is what will let you know that you have to pay attention and sort what all is happening. When you receive that signal, you need to stop, take a step back, and assess what is going on.

If you make this congruence check a habit when you are looking at your dreams and goals, you will become less likely to find yourself in situations where you are in conflict with others and yourself.

Understanding the incongruence that other people may have will make it easier for you to accept this as a normal thing. You only have to seek out clarification of their incongruence by asking them for a reason behind their less than enthusiastic look when they provide you with a positive reply. You should want to understand why they are incongruent as there could be something else that will need to be handled.

We won't all be congruent with every single person that we come in contact with. The way we act when we are with our female friends is going to be different than how you act around your male friends. The way we act around our parents, doctor, teachers or even a cop who pulls us over is going to all be different.

We are all made up of different parts and those parts will be used for every situation that we find ourselves in when we meet a person. When every working part is connected into a whole, we are working congruently.

- Disassociated or Associated

Remember the memories that you recalled for the congruence checklist? You likely have noticed that you were emotionally impacted in different ways in both situations. In the first memory, you were "in" what happened. In NLP, this is known as an associated experience. In your second memory, you were "outside" of the memory and observing what happened. This is what is known as a disassociated experience.

Using the technique of disassociation and association is extremely useful. When you are associated with an image or a memory, no matter if it's imaginary or real, it will be a lot more intense. When you are disassociated from a memory, you watch yourself in it, like a movie. You get information from that moment, but you won't experience an emotional impact.

When you can recall an experience in a disassociated way, you will be able to be an impartial judge. Think back to your two memories. The first you were associated and felt everything. In the second, you were disassociated and observed everything from the outside. Everything was "over there." If there is a memory that makes you feel yucky, then you should always visit it disassociated. There is no reason to feel all of those bad feelings again. You can get information out of it by viewing it as a movie. There are a lot of powerful ways to deal with really traumatic memories.

Secret Driving Habits

Your driving habits are the moments that take you from point A to point B. Most likely, these are strategies that you have created over the years, unconsciously. The ability to change up the process that you experience your reality tends to be more valuable than actually changing the content of your experience of reality.

A strategy is a sequence of steps that you take to perform a certain task. These are your driving habits. It's important to know that a strategy is not the same thing as a behavior. Strategies are unconscious, therefore they become a decision-making process that happened before you were even aware of the external stimulus. In fact, that moment of awareness will typically coincide with the strategies output.

For example, if you don't like spiders, then your strategy has been completed long before you are even aware that a spider is in the room. Your strategy is the decision process you go through, and when you model talented people, it is the decision they make that you have to value.

Pretty much anybody is able to mimic a behavior. The main thing that marks the difference between average and exemplary performance is being able to make decisions that help create that behavior.

Driving a car is made up of a simple behavior set. Your hands and your feet move up and down but knowing when you should do this and how much, is what makes you able to drive. When you started driving, all you did was go through the motions. You didn't make any decisions about where you were going, how fast you wanted to get there, when you stopped or started, and when you turned. The only thing you could manage to do was operate the car. Everything else was above your competency. As you became accustomed to the mechanical movements, you were able to relax and concentrate on the world around you. You soon realized that there were other cars and people out there and that the road could be a dangerous place. You have to learn how to navigate the different obstacles. Most of the learning process is mental and not mechanical. We aren't able to see a person do the mental part, though. We have to assume that playing football, driving a car, or practicing Tai

Chi are all physical skills. They are actually physical movements that were manifested from a complex mental process.

Your strategies, then, are a habitual decision that will result in a course of action based upon a specific stimulus. If you were to come up with a skill for goal setting, it could be made up of:

1. A visual view of what you want.
2. A bodily check for congruence with the outcome.
3. A visual recall of the current situation.
4. A visual view of the steps that need to be taken for the outcome.
5. A bodily check for congruence with the outcome.

Basically, a person will imagine what they want to have, they feel good about it, they imagine what they have to do to reach it, and if it still feels good, they act upon it.

The TOTE model was created in 1960 as an extension to the Stimulus-Response that was created by researchers like Pavlov. Basically, what it means is that you have an unconscious way of knowing that you should start something, a way of knowing to continue it, and a way to know when to stop, and then you can stop thinking.

The TOTE model will provide another layer of formality to your basic strategy because it gives you criteria for beginning and ending your strategy. TOTE means Test Operate Test Exit. TOTE is basically the start and stop points for your strategy. You understand that you should shake hands with a person you have met and you see they have their hand outstretched, and you understand that you should stop when the handshake is finished. You can easily see different strategies working when that other person holds your hand for a bit longer or your hands don't make a good connection. You may even have an experience where you shook hands with a person who didn't intend on shaking your hand.

To make things easier when it comes to writing down a strategy, you can use the following notation:

- V – Visual
- At – Auditory Tonal
- Ad – Auditory Digital (language)
- K – Kinesthetic
- O – Olfactory (smell)
- G – Gustatory (taste)
- I – Internal
- E – External
- C – Constructed
- R – Recalled

VI indicates that there is a mental image that could be recalled like a picture of a recent night out or it could be constructed like a picture of you on a night out in the future. External stimuli happen in real time and can't be recalled or constructed. This provides you with an important distinction when it comes to understanding meta-programs. This is specific to the idea that every meta-program has context specific results of external or internal focus of attention. Here is an example of a strategy using the notation from above:

Oe > OiR > ViC > Ki

This shows that the person smelled something in the outside world that made them remember smelling something. Then they internally visualize and experience and then experience a feeling about this and create a conclusion or a judgment.

A strategies exit or conclusion is most often an internal notion. You will often hear people describe this moment when they say something feels right, or they experience a gut feeling, or they just knew that it was going to go wrong or right. All of these feelings are a result of the activation of glands and muscles.

For example, you could see something while you're shopping and remember one that you have at home. You then say to yourself, "I could use a new one" and then you experience a desire to buy it. This same structure could apply to you seeing an apple and then comparing it to an internal apple representation. You then say to yourself, "This is a nice looking apple." This makes you want to eat it.

Strategies, for everybody, tend to be consistent in several different contexts. After all, why should we waste our time learning a new strategy? Life is basically very conservative and as humans, we like to stay consistent, so to elicit a strategy is one context that tends to be valuable for different contexts. The only way to test a strategy is through consistency. If a person is able to get the same result without the need to think about something, the strategy is working perfectly and their behavior is working correctly because they are getting what they want. Keep in mind, each behavior is started with a positive intention and is meant to achieve something. Whether it ends up being good or bad will all depend on the context.

There is a problem when we represent behavioral decisions this way. How are you supposed to know if this is indeed a person that you need to shake hands with? Do you know this person? Is this a social thing? Has anybody else shaken their hand? Is your hand sticky? Do you have a glass in your hand? Are they interested in meeting you? Once you have started to shake hands, how many times should you shake it? How long should you hold it? When do you need to release their hand? How do you let their hand go?

Even a simple thing as shaking a hand can be broken down into several different decision points that would be very hard to represent in a TOTE flowchart. In order to understand your behavior for a certain strategy, you have to assume a lot of things.

Development and Learning

One great way to understand how people are able to learn is to understand how the brain and mental abilities are created. Scientists, through experimentation, can deduce how children are able to see the world in a different way than many adults. This way we are able to see the stages of learning from various angles.

Children tend to take a long time to reach full mental maturity. As a species, humans are unusual in that human babies can't fend for themselves right after they are born. Several other mammals are able to walk and stand within minutes of being born, but since a human has a large head, a baby has a brain that hasn't fully developed.

Our mental capacity also comes at a cost. We have an extended development time once we are born. This is when we are extremely vulnerable and have to be protected by our parents. There must be several months of learning before the baby is able to do things that a calf or lamb can do right after they are born.

Psychologists are able to use this extended developmental period to study the way children learn, how they view the world, the way they think, and how they develop. Jean Piaget, a Swiss scientist, conducted large amounts of research and came up with several developmental stages that child will most likely progress through, and this created the basis of a lot of child psychology and developmental testing.

Children live in a sensory world. Play a game of "peek-a-boo" with a baby and you will notice that the baby is delighted and surprised every time they see your face. How come the baby is surprised over and over again? Surely, they should know that the face is still there but was hidden from their sight. In fact, a baby's worldly experience is so concrete and built upon their sense, when they can't see something, to them, it no longer exists.

As they age, they will explore and start to create "maps" of their surroundings. There will come an age when a child isn't surprised by your reappearing face and you will notice a different behavior. When you hide your face or a toy, the child will start to try to find it.

The child has a conflict in data. They think the toy doesn't exist anymore, but past experience tells them that the toy is only out of sight. The child will then try to resolve this problem. Between the ages of four and 12 months, the child will begin to use their internal map and they will value their own internal data with the external data.

Several years later, while at a magic show, that delight and surprise will be rekindled when a child tries to find the ball in the magician's hand, but it turns out to be empty. The more you allow the child to be exposed to sensory experiences, the more information they will have to create maps and create new ways to view their world.

Let's quickly go over the developmental phases of a child:

- Sensorimotor: zero to two years

This is during the time the child is developing their sensory awareness and motor skills. They learn how to sense the world and take action to meet their needs.

- Pre-Operational: two to seven years

This is when the child will learn how to use symbols to represent real-world events and objects. Symbols are used to represent something and you can have lots of symbols that represent one thing. The child will start to develop a sense of the past and future. This will mark their progression into their next development stage.

An important abstract map that a child will learn is language. Language is a symbolic representation of their world. Once a child has learned to use the symbol, they will be able to communicate their needs to those around them. Children will learn several different symbols so that they can communicate and parents will have differing success levels of being about to interpret their symbols.

- Concrete Operations: seven to eleven years

Operations here refer to logical rules or calculations that can be used to solve problems. The child will be able to understand symbols and change those symbols to figure out problems. At first, this is still going to have to be within the context of real-world situations. When children are taught math at this phase, they will likely do better using objects than purely abstract ideas. About age six is when most children will learn the quantity of something and will remain constant even if the size and shape of a container are different.

- Formal Operations: 12 plus years

The child has started to develop adult thinking abilities, especially the ability to use abstract operations and logic and they will form theories about the way things work.

Once you have a full appreciation of the way the mind develops, you will start to see how learning is a process that is able to be copied and studied. No matter how old we are, what job we have, or our social status, we all have our life to share experiences.

Before we dive headfirst into NLP modeling practices, we need to make sure that you understand a thing or two about learning. Learning is a natural process that modeling tries to unpick and replicate. When you understand the learning process, you will notice that it is easier to use the models.

While most people will spend their entire life learning more and more about their craft, it shouldn't take them a lifetime to master one specific skill in their craft. Most of the learning time will be redundant; working on motor actions instead of actually learning decision criteria or doing things that have an effect on that skill that you want to model.

While there may be several theories out there about learning, representing all of the different ways that you are able to analyze the subject, the one we are going to look at is Kolb's theory because it shows you a cyclical learning process instead of a static one. David Kolb published his learning model in 1984. This was called Kolb's experiential learning theory. He divided the learning cycle into four stages:

1. Concrete Experience

This stage is the visceral, first hand, direct, physical, and real sensory experience. One experience could be made up of any combo of smells, tastes, feelings, sounds, and sights. You might even know that every experience and memories are made up of every element, even though some are likely to be less prominent than others. These concrete experiences are external and will happen in the present.

2. Reflective Observation

After a person has had a concrete experience, they will reflect upon it. The mind is cast back, both unconsciously and consciously, and then relives the experience so that they are able to create generalizations and create conclusions. Research has found that the brain structure called the hippocampus will make an "action replay" of events that were emotionally charged. This will etch them into our long-term memory. Reflective observation is internal and is always in the past. The observation may not always be visual, it uses the sensory information that was there when you had the first experience.

3. Abstract Concept

Once you have relived the experience, you will take the conclusions you have drawn and use them to make an abstract concept. This is a set of principles or rules that govern that experience any other ones like it. When this process involves mental rehearsal, it will be internal and happen in the future, but it is actually a replay of the past that you aren't able to internally represent in the future, so it doesn't exist yet.

4. Active Experiment

Lastly, the abstract concept will be tested by applying it to a new situation. A child will do this by testing out objects they find out the house to see if they float as their balloon did. A man gives the plants in the house a close trim so that he can try out his hedge trimmer that he got as a present. This active experimentation will bring you full circle to a new concrete experience. This will either contradict or affirm the abstract concept. Active experimentation is external and always in the present.

There are some NLP practitioners that would let you think that a model is able to be installed in just a few seconds, but this tends to be unrealistic. Studies on brain plasticity and learning have found that a realistic time to program in a new behavior will take around six months when you practice it daily, reflect, and integrate. It's interesting to see that the most advanced and current work in neuroscience adds more weight to what teachers have been telling us for years now. Students need to have regular practice over a long time period along with proper rest so that they can truly master a skill. Getting a good night's sleep is a part of this learning process.

One common way to approach learning is to have the sequence of activities structured like this:

1. Come up with a theory.
2. Locate practical examples of it.
3. Use this theory to create a personal concept.
4. Apply your personal concept.
5. Reflect on your experience to create a new theory.
6. Repeat the entire process with new, and maybe contradictory, theory.

A student who is studying may learn about Jung's theory of archetypes. They could look at the descriptions and locate real-life examples of people they know that fit into those descriptions. They could use a psychometric instrument or indicator tool to bring their experiences into the process of learning. They would then figure out how they could use this theory in their work and practically use it.

After some time working on the theory, they may reflect on the things they have learned, how it can be practically used, and about their own experiences and preconceptions. They would abstract those experiences and make a new model.

Perspective

There is a famous adage you will likely hear when using NLP: "The map is not the territory." All this means is that you can't understand reality. The only thing that you are able to truly understand is your perception of reality which is based upon your perspective.

Perspective is the thing that gives you an understanding of the world. One person could see the world from one point of view and come up with one perspective. Looking at it from a different point of view, another person will likely come up with a different perspective. This is the same thing that happened to the six blind men and the elephant. This story comes from Wil Dieck's book, *Ordinary People, Extraordinary Lives: The Convergence of Mind, Body, and Spirit.*

These six men lived in a hut in India. A little boy came into the village one day and ran into their hut and told them, "There's an elephant in the village!" The blind men were interested in learning what an elephant looked like since they had never seen one. They all held hands and the boy led them to the elephant that was calmly standing in the middle of the village. The elephant was eating some veggies that the villagers had brought him.

The blind circled him. The one in the front felt the elephant's trunk. He thought the elephant looked like a tree branch. The next man felt its ears and said the elephant was like a fan. The third man felt the elephant's leg. He thought the elephant was like a pillar of the temple. The next man felt the tail and said the elephant was only a tiny tree branch. The fifth felt its side and said the elephant was like the temple's walls. And the last was rubbing the tusks and said that the elephant was a sharp spear.

These men argued loudly. Soon, they started to disturb the villagers. Finally, one of the old men in the village told them to stop. He told the men to move around the elephant and feel all of the elephant.

They respected the man, so they did as he said. Every time they moved, they each experienced a new part of the elephant. This gave them all a different perspective. They were each able to experience things from each other's perspective.

Much like the blind men, you are going to experience the world through your own senses. The information that you receive will be turned into usable data through neurological functions. This data will allow you to make your own reality map. The problem with your map is that you will only see your own reality.

Using NLP, you will be able to examine your map so that you can figure out if your view is accurate, or at the very least, suitable for you to use. If you find that it's not, you will be able to use NLP to change your map. These types of adjustments will give you control over the way you experience the world. It will also provide you with the chance to help others view things from your point of view.

Throughout your life, your mind has created shortcuts that help you to understand the world around you. All of these shortcuts control your focus. The focus is what controls your purpose. These shortcuts are sometimes good, like when you stop a red light or when you look both ways before you walk across the street. Sometimes the shortcuts aren't good. You may hear a song that reminds you of a sad moment. You get the smell of sugar cookies and then you feel like you have to eat one. Of course, you won't be able to only eat one.

NLP will help you to figure out what your shortcuts are so that you can redefine them. This is going to give you better control. You will also be able to identify another person's shortcuts. You can use this understanding to help them redefine theirs as well.

A perceptual position is a way that a person will see a conversation or interaction. When the perceptional position is varied, you are able to change how you see things. It will also help you to get a better view of another person's perspective.

Negotiations are one of the best uses of perceptional positions. Having a good negotiation is only possible if you understand all viewpoints. With any conflict, the solution will need to take a different perspective. This will give you the chance to see the problem from the other person's perspective. After you understand their perspective, you will be able to notice what they want and why they are going after it. This perspective is what will allow you to provide an acceptable alternative.

There are four different perceptual positions to look at. These four will range from seeing something through your own eyes to seeing an interaction as an outsider.

1. The first perceptual position is being fully associated. This means that you and your body are experiencing things as it happens. You are able to feel, hear, and see through your point of view.

2. The second position is that you feel experiences that somebody else has. This is done by figuratively placing yourself in their shoes. From here, you will be able to

think about how that person feels and how they think. This will help you to understand a problem from another person's perspective.

3. The third position is where you observe the interaction or dialogue between the second and first position. From this position, you are able to use what you are witnessing and hearing to create some assumptions about the other positions. This will give you another way to look at their dynamics and relationship.

4. The fourth position is as a mediator. From here, you are able to address the third position. Here you are trying to figure out if there is another concept that will be helpful. From this point, you will also be able to look at the second position so that you can find other understandings of their behaviors and thoughts. This is going to help you to figure out how you could benefit from them.

These positions are extremely important for NLP. They are used to get clear ideas of the several different perspectives that could be used in any situation at any point. As you move along with these positions, you will start to see your beliefs and values change. These different perceptions will let you learn things you wouldn't have otherwise. You will be able to use these understandings to figure out the best solution.

Take Charge of Your Mind

The Rule of Expectations will use expectations to impact reality and get results. People will make decisions on the way they think others want them to perform. Because of this, people will fulfill these expectations whether they are negative or positive. Expectations have impacts on people we respect and trust, but a bigger impact on strangers. If we realize that somebody is expecting something from us, we try to satisfy them to gain likability and respect.

We've all heard the saying: "What gets measured, gets done." This is also true when talking about expectations. What is expected is what will happen. People will do whatever possible to meet your expectations. This force is powerful and could lead to either the destruction or improvement of this person. You might be expressing expectations of skepticism, lack of confidence, or doubt and you will get results. If you think highly of a person, show them confidence, and want them to succeed, and you will see results from them. To quote John H. Spalding: "Those who believe in our ability do more than stimulate us. They create for us an atmosphere in which it becomes easier to succeed." Once you have created expectations, you will change a person's behavior. When we label certain characters or behaviors, this action is expected. If these expectations aren't met, you might see dissatisfaction, surprise, disgust, or anger.

We can communicate expectations in many different ways. It could be through body language, voice inflections, or language. Think about a time when you were introduced to a new person. If they give you their first name, you give them yours. If they give their full name, you do the same. You might not even realize it, you are accepting cues from them regarding their expectations and you are acting according to their wishes. We all unknowingly send out expectations and cues. Their power is by using the Rule of Expectations consciously.

Many studies have shown how expectations can influence other's performance in drastic ways. In one study, they told a classroom of kids that no one was going to do well on the test and everyone did poorly on the test. In another study, assembly workers were told their job was hard and didn't perform as well on the same task as the workers who were told it was an easy job. Another study showed adults that were given mazes solved them faster when they were told they were grade school level mazes.

If you can add the Rule of Expectations to your repertoire, you could change the audience's expectations of you and their expectation to purchase your idea, service, or product. When you can do this, you will be a lot more persuasive.

Everyone has heard about the Pavlov's dog experiments. Pavlov used the Rule of Expectations to train his dogs to begin salivating when they heard a buzzer. The Rule of Expectations has been used in advertising to make us humans salivate when we see commercials or think about a specific food.

Expect with Confidence

Sometimes we base our expectations on what we assume about groups of people or an individual person. This is the same with us. You may have noticed how expectations have become a reality in your life. Expectations are a self-fulfilled prophecy. We accomplish this by subconsciously and consciously. If there was a child in school with you who were constantly disruptive and rowdy, people have already assumed them to act in a specific way and that is how they will act. They may not even mean to act this way. This child knew everyone thought he was disruptive and so he became disruptive. His teachers expected bad behavior and their expectations were fulfilled.

Think about the impact this might have in your life. Do the expectations and assumptions you have about yourself victimize or liberate you? There are numerous examples of the Rule of Expectations working each day. Have you noticed a person who thought they were getting fired? Their enthusiasm and quality of work dropped. What happens next? They got fired. Their belief caused them to act in a specific way. Those expectations then work to do the very thing they were worried about.

A study was done with second graders who listened to their teachers before they took a math test. They heard three types of statements — reinforcement, persuasion, or expectation. The reinforcement statements went something like this: "You've done excellent work." "I'm happy about your progress." The persuasion statements said: "You need to get better grades in math." "You should be good at math." The expectation statements said: "You work hard at math." "You know math very well." What do you think the results looked like? The expectation statements had the highest scores. Why were these most effective? They gave each student personal assumptions. These assumptions conditioned the results.

Expectation Affect Behavior

When we create expectations for others, they usually become reality. This has interesting effects when we apply them to the real world. Let's go over some examples of how expectations can change lives and persuade behaviors of people.

- School Teachers

When talking about expectations, teachers could be the worst negative influence or the best asset for a child. If a teacher labels a student as being a troublemaker, it will create specific expectations on the student's actions. Labels such as "ADD", "stupid", "slow learner" can become projections on a child's future success. I remember a story about a substitute teacher who received a note from the normal teacher telling her about that there was one student who always caused trouble and another who was very helpful. As the substitute started class, she looked for these students. Once she found them, she treated them as their labels stated. Once the teacher came back, it amazed her that the substitute found the troublemaker was very helpful and the helper was a troublemaker. The substitute mixed them up. The children behaved based on the substitute's expectation. This is also referred to as social labeling. People will live up to either the negative or positive label that gets put on them.

Everyone has had teachers who expected great things from us and brought us to another level. Can you even imagine how powerful this can be? Think about the first day of class while the teacher is looking around the room. Let's say she has a student who is the offspring of a well-known Asian professor, another one is the sister of a former class clown, and one who has many piercings and is wearing nothing but black. You can probably imagine what her expectations and assumptions were. Her expectations will be fulfilled without even talking to any of the students.

One experiment shows how the teacher's expectations can influence students. An elementary school chose two Head Start teachers who were equals in practice and potential. Then, the classes were formed by students who had been tested to make sure they were very similar in learning potential and background. The principal talked to the teachers alone. He gave the first teacher a pep talk and told her she was very fortunate to have a class of very potential students for the year. "Don't get in their way, let them run." The other teacher was told her students weren't very bright but to do the best she could with them. At the conclusion of the school year, the classes were tested and it wasn't surprising to find the first class scored higher than the second. The only factor that was different was the teacher's expectations.

- Grubby Day

Most schools will have days where students were allowed to dress up for Halloween, Fifties Day, Pajama Day, or Spirit Day. One high school had a day labeled as Grubby Day. As you might have guessed, during this day, student's behaviors were not very outstanding. The administrators received more complaints on the student's behaviors during this day than any other. This dress code set up specific assumptions that set up specific expectations. These expectations became fulfilled by bad behavior.

- Littering

Most children will always drop their trash on the floor. One elementary teacher gave her students individually wrapped pieces of candy. The majority of the wrappers wound up on the floor instead of the garbage can. During the next few weeks, the teacher made a point of telling her students how tidy and neat the students had been. The principal came to visit this class and commented on the fact that this class was the cleanest and neatest in the entire school. The janitor even wrote a note on the chalkboard and told the students how clean their room was. When the two weeks were up, the children were given candy again. This time, the wrappers were put into the trash.

- Parental Expectation

The main thing to notice about small children and toddlers is they will behave according to what their parents expect of them. While interning in college and visiting various playgrounds learning about children's behaviors, I noticed that if a child fell down or bumped into another child, they automatically looked to their parent to see how they were going to react. If the parent showed pain or concern on their face, their child would begin to cry to get attention. This happened whether or not the child was really hurt. Any time my daughter would fall around my mother, my mother would automatically fall apart and my daughter would begin to cry uncontrollably. It didn't matter if she was hurt bad or not. The crying began and it would take a long time to get her calmed back down.

A technique I tried was opposite of this approach. I changed expectations and it worked wonderfully. If my child hit her head or scraped her knee, she looked at me and I would ask her if she was bleeding. When she looked at her injury and didn't see blood, she would smile and continue playing. If she saw blood, she would become concerned but we would wash it off, bandage it up and she would be playing again in a matter of minutes.

Children will always live up to their parent's expectations whether these are negative or positive. Most of the inmates in prison were told by their parents while growing up, "You are going to go to jail." Guess what, they did.

- Blood Drive

Blood drive organizers will make calls to remind donors to come in. They usually end their conversations by stating something like, "We will see you in the morning at ten am, okay?" They will wait for the person's commitment before they hang up. Why do they do it this way? Studies show when you make an expectation toward someone, the attendance rate will go up tremendously.

- Sales Applications

Power of suggestions is a very effective way to engage emotions into your tactics. When a car salesperson states: "You are really going to fall in love with this car because it can handle these mountain roads very well." He is taking the focus off the sale and creating an image in the buyer's head. He is speaking as they have already agreed on the same since you won't be driving the roads if you haven't bought the car. He is acting as if it is a done deal. The truth of the matter is the more he talks like this, the more it will probably happen.

Salespeople who go door to door have to use this law. They walk up to a door, ring the bell, and plaster a huge smile on their face while telling this potential buyer they have a presentation that they absolutely have to see. They are employing this strategy while wiping their dirty feel on the doormat hoping to be asked into the house. It is surprising that this technique still continues to work. You can see the salesperson giving the purchaser a pen hoping they are going to sign a contract. Have you felt bad when you leave a store and didn't buy anything? The store created an expectation that you will buy something.

Your Inner Voice

It doesn't matter what we call it. Some call it wisdom, soul, insight, knowledge, or gut feeling. This is what we all look for.

A simple definition of intuition is "The ability to understand something immediately, without the need for conscious reasoning."

It might be a sixth sense, inkling, feeling, or hunch. It is the way we make judgments and snap decisions. We've all had an intuition, feeling, or hunch and even though there wasn't any evidence to back up these feelings, data and science did back up what they already knew to be true.

Most of our brain activity will happen on unconscious levels. Studies show that five percent of our cognitive activity like behavior, actions, emotions, and decisions will come from the conscious mind.

We take in information through our senses every second of every day and we process it all at very fast speeds. That voice, sense, inkling, hunch, intuition is coming from loads of information that we can't consciously or cognitively process.

A simple definition of cognition is "The mental action or process of acquiring knowledge and understanding through our senses, experiences, and thoughts."

This is talking about organizing, discernment, problem-solving, and understanding. This is the thinking and logical part of our brains. We constantly weigh cons and pros, coming to rational conclusions that are based on factors or data. These are the voices that try to override our instincts.

What if I Don't Hear Voices?

Your inner wisdom isn't always a voice you hear. Sometimes it might be an emotion, energy, image, sensation, or feeling. You might feel it in your body. There is no right or wrong way to experience this inner voice. The main thing is to figure out where and when you feel it.

- Gut Feeling

Do you feel it in your gut? You might have heard our guts are our second brain. This is due to the enteric nervous system. It operates separately from the spinal cord, brain, and central nervous system. Yes, you can think with your gut.

Marisa Peer has stated: "The stomach is the seat of all emotions and your feeling are the most real thing you have; so the trick is to listen to your feelings. If something feels wrong, your inner voice is saying it is not right for you. If you get the horrible lurch in your stomach, your inner voice is telling you it is wrong."

- Heart

I asked a good colleague and friend who has always had a good sense of self-awareness where her inner voice is, she replied: "My heart. It is always my heart." This isn't surprising since our hearts are intelligent organs.

Many people don't realize that our hearts can decide, think, and feel for itself. It has about 40,000 neurons and a complete network of neurotransmitters that have very specific functions. This makes it the perfect extension of your brain. It is automatic like a primal, mysterious voice is telling us that the center of our conscience and true being is located there.

- Head

When talking to a male friend about their inner voice, they balked at the idea of the feeling being in his heart or gut. He told me that his inner voice was always in the back of his head that will talk to him and not with him.

Dropping Anchors

Everybody has been faced with a mound of work to accomplish and you end up feeling lazy and overwhelmed. You find it hard to kick-start your mind. The problem is that we view our workload in a boring light. Because we associate it like this, our body will respond by slowing down out actions and creating a sleep-like state. This will cause you to get lost in doing something else and your work will continue to pile up.

We have the power to change our body's response to a thing by changing our emotions associated with that task. This will make us more productive. This technique is referred to as anchoring. This method will recall previous positive experiences and associate it with what is currently happening.

Anchoring can be used in several situations — at work, during a presentation, moments before an interview, during a performance, meeting a person, going on a date, and so on. You can view it as copying and pasting a positive emotion that you need. This can be done first thing in the morning to prepare you for your day.

1. Mental prep

Find a quiet place. Peace is important, so distractions should be eliminated to reap the most benefits. Relax and allow your heartbeat to slow. Cancel out the out world and close your eyes.

2. Recall a previous positive experience

This can be anything as long as that moment makes you feel good when you think about it. Take ten seconds to remember all of the details. This will normally work better when you can use all five of your senses. Think about what you heard, felt, smelled, the other people around, and what you looked at.

3. Associate with an action

Keep this memory in your mind. As you do this, perform an action. The easiest action is to squeeze the thumb and index fingers of your right hand. While you do this, increase the feelings that are flowing through you. Make sure that you make the picture vivid and alive.

This is what is known as laying the anchor. When you recalled your event, you use neurological components that created emotions to come up. By squeezing your fingers, you created a bookmark in your mind. Now you will associate that finger squeeze with a happy memory.

4. Repeat

Take a few minutes and perform your action at least five times more. You want to make sure that your mind quickly connects the action with your happy memory. With practice, that squeeze will flash an image of happiness into your mind.

5. Use your anchor

Before you do something that you are dreading, you can use your anchor to provide you with confidence to do well. When you do use your anchor, increase those feelings and then quickly break your state once the memories are at their peak. By cutting off your anchor right before it peaks, the energy will hang around. Open your eyes and you will notice a surge of positivity.

Breaking state can be done by doing a random act like looking at something around you or reading a text.

Another way to use anchors is to replace a negative emotion with a positive emotion. Remember, you need to practice this method and the one before to get the best results.

1. Anchor your negative memory

Like before, relax, close your eyes, and recall a negative experience. You want to make it real, but not overpowering. Too much power could make things worse. Use a gesture on your left hand to create the anchor. Recall this anchor a couple of times to make sure that you can feel this negative moment. Break your state for 30 seconds.

2. Use your positive anchor

Try to think of a moment that had you feeling the opposite of your negative anchor. This is where you need to focus. Increase this memory. Let this moment meditate in your mind for 30 seconds. Try to remember every little detail. Create an action on your right hand for this anchor.

3. Test your positive anchor

When you perform the gesture for the positive anchor, you want that mental image to become huge. You want your emotions to intensify. Let everything else go and let those feelings consume you. Do the step two to three times then break state.

4. Collapse the anchors

This is tricky and will need some practice. Your positive anchor needs to have a more intense effect than the negative one. Take a deep breath and relax. When you're ready, activate both of your anchors at the exact same time. It's going to feel weird because your brain won't like feeling these contrasting emotions together. Since your positive anchor is more intense, it is going to overpower your negative one and cause it to collapse. After the positive state has taken over, hold onto it for ten seconds. Open your eyes and you will notice a surge of positivity.

Dissociation

A powerful controller is an association-dissociation pattern. You want to take a vacation but you need to save up some money first. What will make you save money?

- Association

You think about your destination as a movie. You see it in 3D and it feels like you can reach out and touch it. You hear sounds and music. You hear a rhythm. It feels like you are really there, seeing it with your own eyes. Deep down there is a fear. When we get overwhelmed with emotions, dissociating is a great relief.

- Dissociation

You are thinking about your destination but only see a small black and white photo. You may see yourself there instead of seeing it with your eyes. This inner voice tells you "I guess it might be nice."

- Using Association Dissociation

This pattern is an important submodality distinction. When we are associated, we relive an experience and feel all the feeling. When we are dissociated, we see ourselves. The feelings we have are about the experience. This is not the same thing as the mental health "Dissociative Disorders".

- When to be associated

If you are remembering or experiencing something pleasant, it would be great to be associated. It is a necessary part of learning a new skill such as a physical activity like sports. It's a great way to get motivated and to enjoy activities.

- When to be dissociated

It is more useful to dissociate yourself from unpleasant experiences and memories. How can you get motivated to do a time consuming or unpleasant task? You have to view yourself doing everything associated with the task and follow it through to an end result. Focus on feelings of a task well done.

- Making life miserable

Most people will do the opposite. They will continuously experience unpleasant events or memories in a way that you experience all the bad feelings. They will remember good events in a totally disconnected way. It is horrible to do something fun but you aren't experiencing all the joys of it. You are thinking about your taxes.

Content Reframing

Content reframing refers to a consciously directed form of a positive attitude that will enable you to get the best outcome from the worst situations. It gives you the chance to reframe the content of a negative moment into something more positive.

To help you learn how to reframe, we're going to look at a common occurrence, the unexpected loss of a job. When you lose a job, everything will look bleak. It may not be all that easy to find another position. While all of this happens, you still have to face the realities of life.

But you can look at this in a different way. Since you are out of work, you know of new opportunities to find a better job. You can explore different skills and opportunities that you may not have thought of before. It will also build character. You will become more courageous, daring, and self-reliant.

With this, you have attempted to reframe your negative event into a positive outcome. It will be surprising to notice all of your blind spots that negative emotions can cause. Content reframing gives you a chance to step back, take a breath, and view your situation from a more objective place.

Content reframing doesn't deny the fact that your situation will be difficult, but you will be more likely to face the situation more successfully if you view it as a moment of growth.

The Art of Persuasion and Manipulation

Meta-programs are the way you internally represent your experiences. They are mental shortcuts or recognition patterns. They work to sort out and prioritize what your body senses. This can help you make sense of the information you have received.

The term meta came from computer science. It is derived from the way a program can control the functions of another program.

Another way to think about meta-programs is in biological terms. Here's an example: Hormones that are produced in the pituitary gland can control the hormones that are produced in various glands in the endocrine system.

Meta-program is a way of thinking that changes how you look at reality. These can control your focus, actions, behaviors, and decisions.

These are processes that are subconsciously in your mind. They manage and direct other processes that happen at either meta or elevated levels.

Our brains can use strategies for decision making and being convinced of things. These are internal processes and mental representation that get made up from input from the five senses.

When making decisions, a person might go through several unconscious thoughts such as first you might see images of different options. Second, after you have had time to examine them, you may see that some have possibilities. Then you can choose one that feels best to you.

This is called "kinesthetic, auditory-internal, visual-constructed" in NLP talk. This happened because you saw the image visually and then figured out how you felt about it.

Somebody else could have feelings for each choice first and then see how each one might be implemented and figure out which one they want. Practitioners of NLP call this sequence: kinesthetic is when you feel the choices; visual-constructed is where you see the choices working and then auditory-internal is where you tell yourself the choice.

If two people use the exact strategy, they might come up with totally different results. One person could come to a decision. The other person could feel overwhelmed and confused and not make a decision.

Meta-programs were created from trying to discover what created different responses. Because the internal process is the same, the differences were thought to come from outside sources. These sources were "meta to" the internal process.

What causes this to happen? Our brains are constantly taking in infinite numbers of sensations. Our conscious mind is just capable of being aware of around seven items at any one time. Our brains would be completely overwhelmed if we were completely aware of every single thing at one time.

But all this can lead to other problems. What parts of specific data needs to be selected? What should we pay attention to right now?

In order to work effectively, our minds need to sort out and select just one thing from all the things we are receiving. This is called sorting.

This brings us to another question. How do our subconscious minds make the choices that will give us the best option at that moment?

Habitual Thinking

There are two facts when talking about thinking. One, most of our thinking is habitual. Two, we filter out most of what we receive. To be truthful, most of the input will get no attention at all.

Do you need proof? At this moment, what does the blood that is flowing in your right arm feel like? You hadn't paid any attention to it until this very moment.

Most of the time, just like your arm, filtering is good. What do you do if your subconscious is choosing the wrong information? Information that isn't beneficial at this very moment in time?

What if the meta-program is filtering something that might be helpful, things that you could really use?

If you can gain access to your meta-programs, what would it feel like? Would you be able to make more informed and better decisions and choices?

Scientists first assumed that these programs were already hard-wired into our brains. Others wanted to see if NLP could be used to change them.

Research has shown that meta-programs can be changed by mapping experiences together. They figured out a process that let people "try out" this new program before making it a new habit. By doing this, we only adopt changes that were compatible with other aspects of the personality.

Meta-Programs of NLP

It depends on which expert you ask as to how many meta-programs NLP has. One scientist identified 60, another 51. Don't worry, we are only going to cover four.

- To or Away

This program answers the question of what motivates a person. Is it pleasure or pain? Do you move to feelings of pleasure or away from pain? You could also think about this as where our attention is directed. Is it to what you want or away from what you don't want?

Use this to look at yourself. Do you move toward pleasure or away from pain? If you are a person who moves away from, you think about things in the perspective as to what needs to be avoided. Threats energize you. After you have read an article on diabetes, you might think, "If I don't lose weight and cut back on sugar, I'll become diabetic." This focus causes you to take action by moving away from the pain of getting diabetes.

You get motivated through ways to reach your goals. Think back to the article on diabetes. You will now tell yourself, "If I can improve my weight by exercise and diet, I will be healthier." You aren't moving away from diabetes but you are pushing yourself to good health.

A good way to understand a preference is the way you approach a problem. If you are an away person, you will express and think in terms of what you don't want. If they are asked what you want, you will probably answer like this: "Well, I don't want that to happen and I don't want this. I know this isn't going to help me either."

You are moving away from the pain you are feeling and experiencing. If you are a to person, when someone asks what you want, you might answer: "I would like to feel better, more focused, stronger, etc."

- Frame of Reference

This gives you that answers as to where your motivation comes from. Is it externally or internally? This is called your locus of control.

Your frame of reference will answer this question: "Do you rate your performance from internal standards or do you find feedback from other people?"

If your frame of reference is internal, you get motivation from inside your body. These standards are what you use to judge performance. You usually feel that your outcome is a result of your actions. This is also called an internal locus of control.

If your frame of reference is external, you get motivated by receiving feedback from the world. You use other people's feedback to judge how well you did something. This is called an external locus of control.

If your frame of reference is external, you experience life as it happens to you. You think other people's actions have control over what you accomplish. You find the advice of experts and are influenced by thoughts of others.

- Match Vs. Mismatch

In this program, your attention gets focused on what is different or the same. Do you see things that are similar, alike, or have things in common, or contrast, dislikes, or differences?

One aspect of thinking is our brains are designed to find differences. When we don't notice the same thing happening over and over is called having a habit. This process lets us determine if something hasn't changed enough to grab our attention. By doing this we get to leave it out of our consciousness and focus attention elsewhere.

Being "different" definitely gets our attention. This is because, after thousands and thousands of generations, we figured out that something different could actually mean danger. Being able to see "different" is needed to survive.

We can also see this concept in language. If we would like to express our affection for others, we tell them we "like" them. If we have negative feelings toward somebody, we will say we "dislike" them.

- Possibility or Necessity?

Our behaviors are based on necessity. Others behave based on what could be possible, what might work in their lives.

If possibilities motivate you, you look for the good in the situation. You can see the opportunities. You think you have control and choice about the direction of your life.

If necessity motivates you, you will focus on things you need to do. This may include staying late after everyone has gone home because you feel like you "have to" get all the work done before you can leave. You focus only on the consequences of what will happen if you don't finish.

When motivated by necessity, a person will just do what they need to. They feel as if they don't have any choices. Their world is made up of constraints and rules.

Think about this, why do certain people apply for specific jobs?

Some will apply due to necessity. They feel as if there aren't any other options for them. This means they have to act in a specific way.

Others will apply just because it makes them feel in control of their lives. This person may be motivated by what they want to achieve. These people don't focus on what they "feel" they need to do.

- Sorting

While using meta-programs, you will be working on sorting things out. Sorting will help you choose things from a large group. When you are working for others or yourself, you will be able to target certain attitudes. These can be found while talking to people.

When using meta-programs, you will get in tune with yourself. You could also use them to understand what makes others tick. This will improve how well you interact with people you meet every day.

Internal Representation

We are aware of what happens around us by using our five senses. When we memorize, remember, dream, or think, we are using these senses. We use these to reproduce information we get from sources. These senses are a medium for input.

This includes our smells, tastes, feelings, dialogue, sounds, and internal pictures. Something comes through our input channels that are:

- Gustatory: This is our taste or the ability to know the difference between salty, bitter, sour, and sweet in our mouths.

- Olfactory: This is smell or the ability to distinguish scents.

- Kinesthetic: This is the external or internal feeling that includes touching something or someone, our emotions, textures, and pressures.

- Auditory: This includes sounds, what we heard, and the way people talk.

- Visual: This includes what we see or how somebody looks at us.

We use these systems or mainly the three most used one of feeling, hearing, and seeing all the time and in everything we do. Some of these we aren't even aware of when we do them. Our minds experience things either unconsciously or consciously by tastes, smells, feelings, sounds, and pictures as our senses see the objective world.

Our internal feelings, sounds, and pictures that all of us experience are very likely to be different because of our individual interpretations. These differences cause us to think differently and have various states of mind. We don't know what others think about us but we always think we know. We might watch the same film and conclude that everyone else will agree that it is boring. This isn't always the case. The main reason is the difference in our thinking preference. They are the different senses we use inwardly.

Everyone has a preference to which sense they use in the outer world, the way to communicate, or the way they think. Some people like pictures and images. They remember faces better than sounds. These people have a visual preference. The other will have an auditory preference as they find it easier to remember names through introductions.

People will unintentionally reveal their preference by using certain words like: "I **see** what you mean" suggests this person has a visual preference. "Your idea **sounds** wonderful" suggests this person has an auditory preference. "These shoes **feel** great on my feet" suggests a kinesthetic preference. A person wanting to purchase a new car will be willing to listen to salespeople, some might want to look through the car, and some feel better if they can feel the car. Everyone unconsciously uses their senses each day. It is normal to have a dominant preference.

Since we use all our senses all the time, external experiences will come to mind through all our systems. Because of a preference or what we like to do, we have senses that are more advanced than others when responding to the world. A football fan that regularly goes to games uses mostly their eyes. They will have a very developed visual system. A person who goes to the movies a lot will use their auditory and visual senses. Thinking normally involves the three primary representational systems, kinesthetic, auditory, and visual, many people will favor one or two no matter what they are thinking about.

We can get many benefits from knowing our representational systems. Basic understanding could enable us to be the master of our own mind. We can gain control over the way we view inputs from the world. This will influence our behavior and feelings in the way we choose instead of being subjected to external influences. If we try to identify and use someone else's primary system, we will actually communicate with them better. When we use a common system, it will enhance and facilitate mutual understanding.

After we have figured out our primary system, we can identify our potential. People that display skills in a certain field will have a well-developed representational system. A person who has a visual preference might take up interior design or painting. A person who has an auditory preference might have a career in public speaking or teaching. A person with a kinesthetic preference might have a choice in being either a chef or hair stylist. A person who has an underdeveloped auditory system may have problems playing musical instruments. Some people are quick to conclude they have no talent for a certain activity when their primary sense just hasn't been developed yet.

An external event comes in by a sensory input channel and gets filtered and managed by our nervous system. As we manage the way we perceive these, we generalize, distort, and delete information according to the processes that help to filter our perception.

Everyone has the same five systems but we all differ in the way we see the world internally. With time, we figure out our unique way of using our mental maps. It is a good way to talk to a crowd using combinations of these systems.

Communication Model

- Deletion

This happens when we pay attention to specific parts of an experience and not others. We sometimes omit or overlook others. If our brains didn't delete some information, we would be facing too much information. You might feel as if you have been overloaded with information.

- Distortion

This happens when we change reality by making changes to our experience in sensory data. An old Indian fable about snake analogy versus the distortion of a rope goes like this: A man walking saw what he thought to be a snake and he yells "SNAKE". When he arrived at the place in the road, he discovered that what he thought was a snake was just a piece of rope.

This is an important component of the Communication Model and is used to motivate ourselves. Motivation could happen when we corrupt, change or misrepresent what comes into our nervous system. This information gets changes through a filtering system.

- Generalization

This is where we draw conclusions about several experiences. You might even know somebody who has experienced something one time and form an opinion based on that one time such as "I hate all Country music because I listened to Taylor Swift and I didn't like the way she sang."

Normally, our conscious mind can handle about seven pieces of information at one time. If it gets overloaded, so we try to oversimplify our attitudes and decisions based on information that didn't give enough evidence. Generalization is common today. Everyone does it. It is the result of digital information that causes overload and takes over our sensibility.

We know several people who can't handle seven. If you want to try someone out ask them to name more than seven products in specific categories. Most people might be able to name two or three products in a low-interest category and around nine in a high-interest category. There is the reasoning behind this.

If we don't delete information, we will have too much information coming in. In fact, you might have heard psychologists say that if we were aware of all the information that came in, we might go crazy. This is why we filter all information.

Generalization is the best way we can learn. We take the information we have and then draw conclusions about these conclusions. The main question is when two people receive the same stimulus, don't they have the same response? The answer is basically we generalize and delete information that comes into one of our five filters. These filters are as follows:

- *Programs*

The first of these filters is Programs. When you know a person's program, you can predict a person's state, behaviors, and actions. Programs aren't bad or good, that is just the way somebody handles information.

- *Values*

Values are basically an evaluation filter. This is how we decide if our actions are bad or good, wrong or right and the way we feel about these actions. Values are arranged in a hierarchy with the one that is most important being on the top and the ones that don't matter is lower than that. Everyone has different models of the world. Our values are the result of the way we look at the world. If we communicate with somebody else or ourselves, or if our model of the world conflicts with values whether they are ours or someone else's, there will be conflict.

Values are what we normally move away from or to. This is what repulses or attracts us to something. They are an unconscious, deep belief system about what is important.

Values can also change with context. You may have specific values about what you want out of a relationship and what you want in your business. Your values about one will be different than the other. Actually, if they aren't, you might have trouble with both. Because values are related to context, they might be related to the state.

- *Beliefs*

Beliefs are how we generalize about the world. Beliefs are the way we assume the world to be. Whether it denies or creates personal power. Beliefs are basically our on and off switches. When we are working with somebody else's beliefs, we have to discover what they believe that causes them to do the things they do. We also need to know any disabling beliefs that don't let them do what they want to do.

- *Memories*

Many psychologists say the present only plays a small part in our behavior. They think that as we age, our reactions now are just reactions to collections of memories that we have organized of past memories. We can make changes to our memories to get more positive results.

- *Decisions*

Decisions that we made in our past could create new beliefs or might affect our perception with time. The problem with decisions is that they can be made either at an early age or unconsciously are forgotten. The effect still remains. We can make changes to our decisions.

These filters will determine how we view an event that is happening now. It is the way we represent what puts us into a certain state and physiology. Whatever state we might be in determines our behavior and the communication model determines the way we process information from the world outside.

Three Components of NLP

You can learn more about NLP by focusing on three central components. These are as follows:

1. Subjectivity

Every person will experience the world subjectively. This means that our world experiences make us form subjective models of the way things are. These experiences are comprised of our five senses and our language.

These experiences are formed by our senses of gestation, olfaction, tactician, audition, and vision. By using language, we can think and talk about these experiences. These experiences have patterns that influence the way we view, talk about, and behave in the world.

Our behavior is controlled by these representations. If we can manipulate these subjective experiences, we could possibly change our behavior.

2. Consciousness

Our consciousness branches into two notions —the unconscious and conscious components. Everyone experiences things in our unconscious mind. Our unconscious representation could damage our conscious behavior.

3. Learning

Learning is an imitative behavior and many call this modeling. The theory says that imitative learning could reproduce and code any behavior.

Analyzing Body Language and the Mind

As humans, we are constantly communicating. This could be with hand positions, posture, facial expressions, the tone of voice, words, or if you choose to respond to an email or text message. When you meet a person for the first time, you will probably observe their body movements before they ever speak. At this point, you are sizing up each other. This is so that you can figure out each other's personalities even before you start to talk.

Even though it may be cliché, but actions speak louder than words. Research has found that it takes around four minutes for a person to make their first impression. This means you have a short time period to create a good impression. Surprisingly, you don't have to use your words all that much to create that all too important first impression. Humans will judge each other 55% based solely on body language. The manner of speaking accounts for 38% and the content of their words make up 7%. Even the tone of voice and rhythm is more important than the words that you say.

Before we dive into the different body languages, we are going to quickly look at the way the brain is wired. The brain is made up of two hemispheres. The left hemisphere takes care of the logical data processing. This is what controls the conscious thinking. The right hemisphere is where the emotions are triggered by activity in this area. This hemisphere is also what controls our creativity and intuition.

Since our body is cross-wired, the right hemisphere is what controls the life side of your body, and the left hemisphere controls the right side. This means that any body language shown on a certain side corresponds with the hemisphere of the brain that activates it. Any action that happens on the left side is conscious actions, while actions on the right side are unconscious.

Understanding Body Language

The first stop along the road of body language is facial language. Facial expressions are the first things that a person will notice. A person's mood can be easily noticed depending on how tense or relaxed the facial muscles are. Eyelids even show powerful information.

- Smiling

You can easily notice the feelings using the mouth as a reference point. A smile is typically connected with interest and happiness. A person that smiles too much could be used to hide disinterest. An exaggerated smile shows courtesy or assurance to the speaker to let them know that they are listening even if they aren't. A frown will show dissatisfaction and sadness. Frowning is an unlikely expression when people first meet. This is because we would rather hide our real sentiments instead of being rude. A straight expression or poker face shows neutrality and seriousness. Think about the expression you are interested in giving off the next time that you speak.

- Chin

You can also notice sentiments by checking how they are using their chin. Chin-stroking is a good sign of careful studying. People will often view this as a show of skepticism. Now, if they scratch their chin, it could mean they are confused.

- Jaw and Nostrils

Nostrils are a big indicator of mood or temperament. Heavy breathing with flared nostrils normally means they are angry. It's important that you are aware of these signs. These people should be approached with a soft tone. Don't try to force them to open up when they don't want to. Instead, try giving them some space for a bit before you engage with them again. Another good indicator of their temperament is their jaw muscles. The jaw will normally be in sync with your nostrils. Anger and impatience are typically noticed by the pumping and flexing of the muscles of the jaw.

- Eyes

While eyes are technically a part of facial non-verbal communication, they need to be looked at on their own. Ophthalmic refers to the communication shown by the eyes. This is an effective tool to detect sentiment and mood. People tend to be oblivious to the fact that their eyes share quite a bit of information.

The amount of white you can see under the colored part of the eye, the iris, can reveal how much stress they are feeling at that moment. The white area on the left eye shows the stress the right hemisphere is experiencing. This means that the person could be under stress from the body like lack of food or sleep.

The right eye will show stress from an external source. If the white part of the eye under the iris is revealed after they are exposed to stressful concepts such as overtime and deadlines, the person is likely experiencing discomfort from those things.

Eyelids also show a person's optimism. Watch their bottom lid to see their reaction to your words. If their bottom lid straightens, they are probably skeptical. Once you gain their trust, the bottom lid will round out. This means that they are opening up to you and that you are building rapport.

- Hands and Arms

As we travel down the body, we will start to notice more information about how a person feels. The hands are the main tools for humans, so we will often subconsciously use our hands to express how we feel. These appendages hold more nerves that are connected with our brain than any other body part.

The hands are able to show shyness, anxiety, or restraint if they are being held together. This is due to the energy that is being held between the hands. This is why this is a good way to channel negative energy like nervousness and anger.

If their hands are in the shape of a triangle, the hands are showing deep thinking or confidence. Another variation of this is a rhombus shape where the thumbs are extended out further towards a person. The German Chancellor Angela Merkel is popular for using this gesture. Because of this, the gesture has been given the name the Merkel rhombus that will create a calm yet serious aura.

When you raise your arms with your palms open shows acceptance and honesty. The opposite form shows defiance.

When people give a contemplative look while they use their hands to cover their mouth, they have an idea but they want to keep it to themselves. It helps to encourage these people to share what they are thinking. This could be all they need to make the conversation better.

The manner in which a person crosses their arms will also show their confidence. A partial cross is how a person can unconsciously soothe their own nerves. People who are exhibiting this behavior likely feel anxious. Try easing the mood by making them laugh is some way.

Fully crossed arms will often show that they have an unwillingness to cooperate and work. If they are holding their arms, they are trying to preserve their internal emotions.

- Foot Communication

The feet tend to get ignored when it comes to reading a person's body language. On the contrary, the feet tend to be one of the more candid forms of body language. When people lie, they often hide this by altering their movements. They will focus on their face without realizing their feet are giving them away.

By watching the way that a person sits, you can figure out whether the person is submissive or dominant. Men will normally want to be seen as dominant, this is why they normally take up a lot of space when they sit. They will normally sit with their legs spread apart or in a figure four position. Women tend to be more reserved, so they will cross their legs to take up less space.

Legs will also show a person's sincerity while they are listening. When people want to listen, their legs will point towards the person who is talking with their feet off by a 45-degree angle. However, if their legs are pointing towards the exit, they are not interested in what the person is saying. Make sure you pay attention to the direction of your feet when you are talking.

Reading a person's body language will help you to figure out how to approach them in the friendliest way possible.

Meta Model

How can somebody become better at something? Find a person who is already good at the thing that they want to do and then copy what they do. Modeling is a lot like copying, but copying takes things a bit further. Instead of just copying the observed behavior, it attempts to help a person understand the reasons behind their actions. It's their mental model that will help you to find the same success. Modeling works because it creates a series of templates that are based on things like:

- Physiology
- Body movement
- How people use their language
- All other sensory-related things that a person could notice

This modeling process came about as a result of John Grinder and Richard Bandler's research. The founders of NLP were working to achieve some of the same therapeutic results that Virginia Satir and Fritz Perls were able to achieve. They discovered that they had to do more than just copy their behaviors. They also had to understand their thought processes affected the outcome.

They discovered that those therapists used all of their skills unconsciously. The same is true for pretty much anybody who performs at an extremely high level. This applies to business people all the way to athletes. High performers will not think consciously about what they do. If you ask any of them how they do something, they will likely have a pretty hard time explaining how they did it.

Why is this? Because they've performed these behaviors hundreds of times. They did them so many times that they happen below their conscious thought. They are now automatic. This is why it is almost impossible for the expert to explain their success. This is why modeling is helpful.

Modeling will involve uncovering the things that an expert knows consciously and unconsciously. This is why modeling is so powerful. Models can be used to transfer the successful behaviors, attitudes, and beliefs of one person to yourself. This is what will let you produce the same results.

There are six stages of modeling.

1. Find your model and watch the behavior you are interested in acquiring.

First, you need to find a person who has consistently produced the results you are looking for. For example, you could be interested in modeling a black belt's sparring method. Modeling can be used to duplicate an eloquent public speaker's ability to connect with the audience.

Modeling can also be used for mundane purposes. You could model a person who does a great job at keeping their home clean. You could even model the way that your boss is able to do their "to-do" list. You would also be able to find out why a person stays depressed. The same goes for people who are always frustrated or angry. This knowledge can help you to stay out of this state.

The key is to find a person who is getting a result that you want to produce. They do this in a consistent manner without fail and then you observe the things they do.

2. Unconsciously start to use their behavioral patterns.

In the majority of modeling methods, the modeler will act as an observer. NLP modeling requires that the modeler will step into the successful person's shoes. Through practice and repeated imitation, you will start to unconsciously absorb that person's behavior patterns.

This means that you will fully imagine yourself in their reality. This is done by using what is known as a second position shift. If you remember from earlier, the second position is what lets you focus on what a person does, which are the things that are the most easily seen. This lets you become aware of how they do things. This is done by adopting their thinking. You will start to figure out why they do the things they do. You will try to find the underlying reasons.

NLP will make use of direct observation to figure out their person's behaviors. This is just like how other modeling methods will try to figure out how to outperform the top performer. They will look at their tonality, words, movements, and so on. This gives you the ability to understand how that person creates their results.

NLP modeling wants you to also understand the why and the how. This will help you to understand what's going on in their head. You will be able to copy them in a more genuine way. The successful performer's why and how can be used to mold your behaviors. This is why the second position is so powerful.

3. Start to produce similar results.

As you begin to act out the person's why and how, you will notice that you will get similar results. Since behaviors could be simple or complex, modeling take a few minutes, hours, days, weeks, months, and possibly years. It will all depend on the complexity of what you are looking to learn.

Since criteria are subjective, find a person that can help you to evaluate whether your results are lining up with the model.

4. Fine tune the pattern.

As you work to perform the behavior or skill, you will start to notice that some things aren't needed. These things aren't needed to produce your desired results. This is where you will fine tune the pattern by testing it to figure what you need to have in it and what you don't. This will also be when you check for improvements.

5. Document the model.

After you have fine-tuned everything, you have to be able to describe the things that are going on. This should be done so that anybody who wants to learn and master this pattern can do so. The easiest way for this to be done is to document the model and then tell an eight-year-old. If they are able to understand what you said, then it's clear.

6. Teach the thing that you have learned.

You become good at something once you can teach it to somebody. You take everything that you have documented and help another person learn the skill. If this ends up being difficult, you will have to modify your description. This should be done until transferring the skill to another becomes easy.

The Right Questions

The most powerful gift that humans have in our communication is the ability to ask questions. Sadly, this is an ability that a lot of people will neglect and is a gift that will often remain undelivered in most communications.

Why would I say that asking questions is a neglected ability? Everybody asks questions. We do, but the art of asking questions is more than making a simple statement and placing a question mark at the end. It's more than a persuasion tactic of some kind to achieve your own objective. It's more than just trying to get your point across, getting your way, or discovering an answer that will benefit you in some way.

We often neglect the art of asking real questions, which is using them as a gift. By gift, I mean asking a person a question without a hidden agenda. Questions that don't have an agenda are questions that you ask a person where you don't have a preconceived objective other than to find out more about what that person thinks. These questions will tell the other that you view them as important. It lets them know that they are more important than you are at that moment.

One of our main motivations in life, other than staying safe, eating, and drinking, is that we want to feel important. Think about the things that are motivating you at this moment? Progressing in your career? Changing your career? Improving your skills? Becoming or feeling successful? Becoming a better parent? The majority of the things that drive us are subconscious needs to feel important.

Through asking a simple question, showing interest, or seeking an opinion, you are sending that other person a message that they are important to you.

The only way this is done is through asking questions during a conversation where you leave behind your values and beliefs. Let's look at it this way.

You're talking with a friend and you ask them a question, "What are your plans this weekend?" This is a seemingly innocent question and it could be completely innocent, however, if you asked the question to try to get your friend to ask a similar question, knowing that you have fun things planned, then these questions come with an agenda. This would be a slight form of manipulation.

You could ask them several questions like "How is your work going?" This is a great starter. Then you ask, "Is your boss still giving you problems?" Using the word still implies that there has been a problem and it could make the other person think that they need to have it fixed. If a question has an implication, then it has an agenda. Do you ask this question to get across your own beliefs? Maybe you believe that problems need to be sorted out fast. Maybe your values are coming through. Frank and open communication are important to you.

Then your next question tells everything, "Shouldn't you get something done about that problem? I would challenge them." This may be a question, but are you actually interested in finding out the answer? These types of questions will likely cause your friend to feel manipulated or criticized. You definitely didn't deliver a gift. You have made yourself feel important.

There are certain ways that you can use language that can imply useful measurements, energy, or lengths of time. The following should be seen as a general guide of those things and what you should look out for when conversing with a person.

- Questions with "Why"

With NLP, we try to avoid starting a question with why. This is because it's hard to predict how much detail somebody could respond with. Why is extremely ambiguous. Every concept, idea, or thing is able to be viewed from different levels of abstraction. This means a person can look at the big picture or fine details. If you are to ask somebody, "Why do you have that job?" they would be able to respond with large concepts like monetary freedom and they skip over the smaller details.

Why also has the tendency to come off as negative. If you ask a person why they aren't able to do something, their brain will go through their resources and memories to pull together the reason why they aren't able to do it. This works like a negative affirmation. It will provide them with a long list of excuses and it won't help them move forward.

- Try using "How"

How questions are more likely to help people think outside their head. Why questions make them look inside themselves, but how will make them look outside themselves to find information that they may not have moved before. How is also infinite in the answers it can create.

Let's assume that in front of you stands a 40-foot wall. Try to come up with five creative ways to get over that wall. How can you do it? Since I first asked you for five ways, you likely came up with five, maybe a few more, and stopped. But think about what happens if I were to just leave you with the how questions.

How could you get over the wall? Think until you run out of ways. How else could you accomplish it? How else? Were you able to squeeze out a couple more?

Now you can see the power of a how question over a why questions.

Asking a good question is an art form and more artists will spend their entire lives perfecting their art. The best way to learn how to ask a question without a hidden agenda is to practice. The next time you are talking with a person, try using some of these tips to leave your agenda at the door:

- Get into a curious mindset. Become really interested in finding out what the other person wants to share.

- Listen closely to their answers. Silence your mind and remove your thoughts that you could experience while they are talking. These are normally opinions forming and you don't want to be interested in your opinions. You are to be interested in theirs.

- Wait for them to answer before you come up with your next question.

- Try asking yourself, "What do I need to understand so that I can understand the whole picture?" Take that answer and form it into a question. What other information do you need? Ask that.

- Try to stay away from questions that use the word why. Why will often lead to the person being asked a question to feel like they have to justify what they did. If you ask, "Why do you go shopping in the morning?" They could interpret it as "Why do you feel like you need to shop?" or "Why would you go in the morning when you could go in the afternoon?"

- Believe in the best of that person. In their own right, everybody is magnificent. What is it that you should ask so that you can let their magnificence shine through?

Now that you have a good idea of how to ask the best question, I want to leave you with two more suggestions. When you can't see to figure out what to ask, try one of these options:

"Is there anything that I've not asked you that you believe would be important or useful to let me know?"

And,

"Is there anything that you want to ask me that I haven't explained to you?"

There will almost always be something that the other person will say to both of these questions because people don't like to have this feeling that there is something that hasn't been answered. It will also take some responsibility and pressure off of you to get all of the information out of the other person.

Personal Beliefs

Our personal beliefs have very little basis in facts but are instead formed from a generalization of what we have experienced, perceptions and views of ourselves, the external world and others, and what we hear from different places that we accept as trustworthy, especially when we were growing up. We will also form beliefs from our own environment and the culture we grew up in. These beliefs will hang around if they stay unproven and will stay with us right through our adulthood. However, there are some beliefs that are based on facts. These would include the law of gravity or other laws about the world.

Beliefs will often control our behavior and they exert a lot of influence on our adversity or otherwise. People act based on their beliefs because they believe them to be true. As long as a person believes that they are unable to do something, their belief will remain an inhibition and they won't ever do it. Even if they do give it a shot, their odds of success are low because they have a negative belief. The reverse is true as well. If a person believes that they are capable of doing something and they do it, they will likely have a successful outcome. This is basically a self-fulfilling prophecy.

Beliefs work like a mental filter. You interpret your external world according to your beliefs. Anything to the contrary won't be accepted because they don't support your beliefs unless it's an exceptional quality. Beliefs will dictate the way that you interact with others. For example, if you were to believe that somebody doesn't like you, you will probably avoid them or try to keep from talking to them. In response, they will likely stay aloof and distant and this will confirm your belief even if they don't actually dislike you.

Over time, your beliefs will change. This is inevitable as you grow and are exposed to more experiences and events. These things will change your beliefs. Not only are your beliefs changed, but it will create empowering ones too. Since beliefs influence behaviors and they create a positive result, you will keep them, otherwise, you will likely change them. Sometimes, you can replace limiting beliefs with suitable ones that will improve your life. When you change your inner limiting beliefs, it will make your behaviors change for the better. This affects your life significantly and can lead to more positive changes. Erroneous beliefs will also have disadvantageous implications. That's why it is important that you replace them with something that is appropriate for you.

The more positive beliefs you have, the more freedom you will have. You will find more possibilities and opportunities. Your success will be improved. Through NLP, you are able to create and choose your own empowering beliefs. That way, you will be able to exploit and develop your potential to reach your desires. However, those belief changes might not last if you allow yourself to give up too soon.

Building Connections

A good use of NLP is being able to establish good communication skills. Leading and pacing is a couple of techniques that you can use to develop rapport. For example, if you live in the United States, you will be able to understand this example better. People who live in different regions will talk at different rates of speed. This is also called pace of speech.

A person living in northern states will always talk faster than somebody from a southern state. This could and sometimes does lead to conflicts and misunderstandings. If you live in a northern state, you can build rapport by slowing down your pace of speech to match a person from a southern state. If you can match their pace, you will make them comfortable around you. This is how to build rapport.

Building trust, harmony, and friendships are the way to make better relationships. These are the main components of building trust and acceptance. Having goodwill toward others can make it easy to open up, connect with other, and having great interactions.

Everyone has a certain type of person who they click with naturally and prefer to interact with. If communication between these two people isn't in sync, it would be safe to say, they aren't going to get along. It might still be easy to create strong relationships or rapport with these people.

After you have learned to pace your speech, you can start using rapport. For example, as you continue talking to this person, you lean back. After some time, they do it too. This is leading.

This sounds manipulative, but if you can use it ethically, it is a great tool to improve rapport. When you can improve rapport, you will improve your communication.

If you can use it correctly, you can convey messages that will resonate to others. It can help build communication and reduce conflicts.

Building Rapport

The following are some techniques that will help you build rapport with others. Some might seem a bit silly but they all work well.

- Mirroring

This is such an easy technique. You do it by mirroring their speech patterns and gestures.

Basically, this is mimicking the behavior of whomever you might be talking to. When talking about the law of attraction, people can bond with others better if they exhibit the same traits. First impressions do last. This is why mirroring is an important technique when you begin interacting with others. Mirroring makes it easier to figure out people's energies and to build rapport.

Let's say you are talking to someone and they cross their arms and lean toward you. To mirror them subtly, start by crossing your hands. Now, tilt your head toward them slightly. If they begin talking loud, you will answer them in a loud voice. Continue mirroring their movements such as if they rub their arm, gently touch yours. Make sure your movements remain subtle. You don't want to rub your arm or deliberately copy everything they do. They might think you are mocking them and get offended.

By mirroring the other person, they will subconsciously see that you are both on the same page. Now, you try to get them to follow your lead.

1. Body Language

   If the person you are speaking with is sitting straight, you need to sit straight. If they cross their arms, cross yours. If they tilt their head, slightly tilt yours. Return gestures such as smiles and handshakes to create trust and courtesy. This will make them feel loved and appreciated and will be more willing to open up to you.

2. Facial Expressions

   We have 53 muscles in our face that can make all sorts of expressions. Everyone can speak volumes without ever saying a work. Are their brows lowered or raised? Are they smooth or furrowed? Is their jaw squared off and tense? Is the bridge of their nose smooth or wrinkled? How fast are they blinking their eyes? A normal person will blink about 15 times each minute. If a person is feeling anxious or is lying, they will blink more. If a person is concentrating, they will blink less. When you match their blink rate, you will have access to their physiological and emotional state. This will take time to master. Since our "eyes are the windows to the soul", it would be worth the effort to try.

3. Breathing Rhythms

   How you breathe tells others the amount of energy you are using. If you are breathing slowly, it shows you are relaxed and calm. Breathing fast shows nervousness or anxiety. Which way do you want others to see you?

4. Match Tempo, Rhythm, and Tone

The matching voice is a great tool to use if you work in sales or do cold calling. When you work this way, you can't rely on your body language.

You need to match the other person's tone such as amused, interested, dry, happy, or excited along with the speed at which they are talking. If the other person talks very fast in an excited voice, you need to keep up with them and sound excited too. If they speak carefully and slow, you need to do it too. With practice, this will come naturally.

Being loud shows intense emotions. It shows signs of frustration and anger. Someone speaking very soft shows they are calm.

Pitch indicates the tone of voice. A high pitch means excitement while a low one shows anger. It is like an informal but serious conversation such as a person in sales will always use a moderate pitch.

The rate is how fast you are talking. If your voice gradually increases, it shows you are becoming more intense. Having too many rates shows you are nervous. Disinterest and boredom are also associated with a slow rate.

Quality is the key to being understood. A person's speech habits, articulation, and pronunciation are things you should remember to communicate effectively. If they talk deliberately and slowly, you need to pace them to match their energy level. When matching their pace, you need to be subtle and natural. If you are a slow speaker, you might have to quicken your pace to match the other person.

Silence controls how the conversation flows. You need to match your partner's silence. Being silent will give you the chance to regroup your thoughts and listen.

5. Sensory Predicates

    Many people will favor one of the four sensory-based systems that allow us to understand our experiences and world. Basically, it is the words we use to describe these experiences. It is helpful to see keys that show the person's favored system so you can use similar words to have meaningful conversations. Many people will put all the systems into their vocabulary but will favor one over the others. Here are the four systems:

    Auditory: They will use phrases or words like give me your ear, on another note, tune out, tune in, loud and clear, clear as a bell, resonate, listen, tell, hear, and sound.

    Feeling/Kinesthetic: They will use phrases and words like hand in hand, make contact, get in touch with, heated debate, unfeeling, solid, sharp as a tack, concrete, hard, fuzzy, grasp, feel, and touch.

    Visual: They might use phrases and words like hazy, picture this, an eyeful, paint a picture, short-sighted, focused, reveal, bright, clear, foggy, view, look, and see.

    Auditory Digital: They might use phrases and words like conceive, word for word, pay attention to, make sense of, figure it out, learn, motivate, experience, understand, consider, decide, process, learn, know, and think.

Always use caution when you mirror another person. Never look like a robot and don't do everything the other person does. Begin with posture and move on to body language until you have reached the mimicking stage. When the person you are talking with return the favor, make your movements smaller. Rapport is matching energy to the people you interact with.

- Systemic Processes

Everyone's minds are connected to their environment. All the stimuli you get from the world enter our brains to be interpreted. After, our minds will perceive these stimuli as either positive or negative. If you put a negative view on a situation, it is going to remain negative and you will view it as a mistake until you make the effort to find positive things about it. These perceptions will eventually become a reality.

- Filtering

NLP believes that each behavior has a positive intention. This positive intent might not be clear or make sense to everyone. The person who is doing this behavior, it makes total sense in their reality. This can help to explain why everybody doesn't want the same things in life or doesn't react the same way to what happens in life. This shows we all have different perceptions and no one is either right or wrong.

You might not agree with someone else's reality, you can't judge them. You need to respect and appreciate that they have different values and beliefs. Respect that they perceive, feel, see, and hear the world differently. They aren't going to have the same values or make the same choices.

If you are talking with a person and they suddenly raise their voice, yells, and then disappears into their room, you might think this is totally unacceptable. Just be curious. Look at it from their perspective. Their view of the world and their circumstances might cause them to feel overwhelmed or uncomfortable during the conversation and they felt this was their only option.

Filters get developed by things like your family, values, beliefs, spiritual practices, or assumptions while growing up. If you don't like your habits, beliefs, or filters, you are the only one who can change these.

The first thing you must do is to become aware of whether they are detracting or attracting to your life. These are the way you see the world. It drives your behaviors and emotions. This is your reality. It is unique to you. If you would like to get different results out of your reality, NLP can change these beliefs.

- Cause and Effect

Most people live their lives in effect. This means they blame circumstances and others for their bad moods. Other people have to make them feel good about themselves. You might be thinking that "If my spouse only understood me, I'd be happier." Sorry dear, you are the only person who has the ability to change that. Have you told your spouse how you feel? If not, how are they going to know? You might be resisting because you just think they don't care. If you continue on this path, nothing is going to change.

If you would like to be the cause, you are making the decisions and creating what you want out of life. You don't rely on others to be happy and you know that. You can be supportive and cheer others while moving forward. You can't take responsibility for other people's emotional states. If you do this, you are putting a huge weight on your shoulders that will eventually drain you. When using cause, you take responsibility for your actions both bad and good. You realize the world is full of opportunities and you have choices to achieve what you want out of life.

- Respond While Pacing

When pacing, you have to respond instead of reacting to what other people are doing or saying. You react when you make a negative judgment about what others are saying. Don't try to disguise it, it will make them uncomfortable and they could become very aggressive.

Responding is listening to the other person and then reflecting their words back to them. You have to do this without judging. This can help you be sure you understand what the other person is saying. This lets them know you accept what they have said. It doesn't matter if you agree with them or not.

Once you respond, they won't see you as a threat. This lets them relax. They will be less guarded and it will be easier for you to move the conversation where you would like for it to go.

- When to Lead

In order to lead, you have to be sure the other person is in rapport with you. You have to first use mirroring and matching. Then, move your body slightly. Change your tone and see if they follow your lead.

When they do, then you have taken the lead. If not, go back to mirroring and matching.

The main thing is to pace yourself, try to get feedback from their language pattern and body language. When done correctly, mirroring gets them to create a positive image of you. When you establish rapport, you will be able to lead the way.

- Failing is Great Feedback

Everybody is going to make mistakes and fail. The main thing that separates us is the way we let it affects us either negatively or positively and the way we look at it. With NLP, it is thought that failure doesn't exist, it is all just a feedback. If something doesn't happen the way you think it should, you aren't a failure. It just means you found something that won't work for you. This gives you the opportunity to figure out ways to improve and do better.

Using Your Words and Voice

Language is a powerful tool to help you reach your goals. People that know how to use language skills usually get into positions of power. Especially when talking politics. This involves making a lot of speeches and is connected to persuasiveness. This factor lets you bring others to your viewpoint, interests, and opinions and will subsequently affect their actions. By infusing specific information into phrases, words, or sentences, you can subliminally persuade data and manipulate people. It is easy for our brains to form connections if it has the right conditioning. It can then learn to connect stimulus to reflexes and that could be just one single word. This alone shows how powerful words are. If words are used the right way, it can change a person's opinion about anything by persuasion. They can trigger a person's imagination and could lead to certain thought patterns and affect how well we do specific skills.

Humans have an innate capacity for learning languages. This simply means that when we are exposed to the correct stimulus, we will be a part of the visual-lingual system of recognition. Our brains associate words with specific emotions, meaning, qualities, and objects. We learn to make connections between the given stimulus in the surroundings and a specific work that was provided from the person's native language. Within everyday sentences, there is a level of uncertainty because a sentence might contain phrases or words that suggest meanings other than what the speaker meant. For example look at this sentence: "Flying planes could be dangerous." This might mean that planes when flying are dangerous or flying planes could put you in danger. In certain languages, one word could have several different meanings. In the English language, the word "orange" means a color and fruit. Our brains register every possible meaning for every word or phrase.

These alternate meanings or hidden connotations can be used in many conversations letting a person play the dominant part in all sorts of interactions. In spite of the fact that the brain can recognize which one is the right meaning of the phrase or word. You can use the given situation and environment to find the meaning. It will still register all the possibilities that might apply. Using rapport is a needed part of the whole endeavor along with other factors like tonality and tone of voice that will exhibit the smallest agreement in the person's statements because it lets them relate easier to you. The correct use of body language is also important.

If this uncertainty gets combined with the right body language and gestures to enhance specific meanings, without the listener noticing, the phrase could carry to the unconscious listener a brand new meaning. When making a statement like: "You know whom you can trust in that case" while talking about your subject and while pointing to yourself, you will send a message to the receiver that it is natural for them to trust you even if the original meaning is something completely different.

The main key to achieving persuasion is to get the person to imagine what you want to show them and get them to see the things you want to see. Making some who is close-minded and argumentative to be more flexible, or getting a client to see how good they are going to feel after receiving your company's benefits. The easiest way to do this is as a question using "if-question" like "What would it feel like if you took the option that I am offering you?" What is in question is the actual thing you would like for them to do. This type of question can generate a feeling you would like them to experience or an idea you would like for them to access by triggering their imagination. This is a powerful tool.

Every suggestion, statement, or sentence we hear, could have the ability to create pictures in our emotions and minds. It acts as a trigger for our imagination by picturing the information that we have been exposed to. This, in turn, will generate thoughts based on the information we received. These thoughts will carry the emotion we first generated and it continues until it gives us a conclusion. If the emotion that was transmitted wound up being negative, then the conclusion will be a negative one, too. Because the thought structure that happens from the statement is negative if the listener doesn't reject the statement and the suggestions say so.

If we have reached a certain conclusion about a subject many times, our brain will register that conclusion, as a rule, it will apply to every situation. If a person constantly shows up late for dates, then you will make a conclusion that this person is late always and from that point on, you will expect them to be late and will take measures such as texting them to remind them to be sure they are on time. To flip it around, the person who is getting these messages realizes that they are expected to be late and forms a picture of them being late. This causes them to come to the same conclusions and start believing it and making it come true and this becomes an unconscious rule.

This can also be used to make restrictive rules about a person's abilities. If a person receives a poor grade a couple times in math, they form a belief that they aren't good in math and then this person's skills in math become poor. They will keep this thought from that point on unless they form a new belief that will remove that rule.

Knowledge can also be used to increase a person's skills. If you can understand that there are techniques you can use to control your ability levels, you can change your programming on what you are and aren't good at. You can remove all those negative ruled statements that keep your abilities at bay. You can start putting more effort on specific skills and you will prove that you are good at it and will replace a negative statement with a positive one. Another effective way to improve a specific skill is by using the "power of words". This is using a conditioner to make a trigger for better skill performance. This is similar to what Pavlov did with his dogs. We can train our brains to form connections between a stimulus and being good at a skill of choice.

Words have power because they can influence people indirectly and directly in many different ways. These can be abused and used because they serve to meet a person's interest. It could be a specific weapon, career choice in politics or marketing, or any profession that takes charisma. Linguistic skills are valuable tools that can help you fulfill your goals and help you as a person.

Conflict Resolution

Studies have shown that managers have found themselves in the middle of many conflicts. You might have a different view of the problems or situations than others. You might both believe in different things and it seems like you just aren't going to agree. You might get frustrated since you believe the other person isn't being considerate. You might have teenagers at home that you are always butting heads with. You might even see co-workers who are having a conflict but don't know how to help them. The conflict might sometimes feel like a contact sport. You might be a person who likes to stay away from conflict because you worry about what might happen. This might mean you completely ignore it, let it come to a head, and then sacrifice yourself in the end.

It would be great if you could just take some easy steps and be able to increase your ability to resolve conflicts. Would you like to understand the reason behind the conflict? If you experienced a conflict and you had tips to help you manage it better and are able to move beyond it, wouldn't it be great? Would you like to help others people who are experiencing conflict? How would it feel if you could recognize and take the steps to resolve that conflict before it affects you negatively?

Ignoring conflict is the worst possible thing you could do. A simple definition of conflict is "a disagreement or clash", "a state of disharmony between incompatible interests or ideas", "to be at odds with". If you put your hat into it, it could escalate it from a minor frustration into a monumental problem. You have to deal with it proactively and positively.

What causes conflicts? Many things such as power struggles, jealousy, pride, having a bad day, competitive tensions, and egos can all cause conflicts. Many conflicts are created from two things — emotions and poor communication.

- Poor communication: Is it not having any information, poor information, misinformation, or lack of information? You might have gotten all the information you need in the correct time frame, the problem is you aren't sure how you can process it. Some information might be missing and when you try to add two plus two, you wind up with ten. You add up information, make assumptions, and generalize to make sense of what you have been given. We can probably all relate to this. Remember that communication is more than just words. There is around 55 percent of the communication will be non-verbal. This is body and physiology language. About 38 percent is tonality and seven percent is actual words.

- Emotions: As some may know, emotions can drive the agenda. The challenge is when our emotions take over the driver's seat. If you remember the conflict, you can see where the emotions took over. Were you able to resolve the conflict successfully? Many executives let their emotions take over and lead to irrational thoughts, things getting said that was totally exaggerated, etc. If you have witnessed somebody in a rage, that does or says something that if they weren't enraged would never have said. Emotions that are overindulged during conflict situations don't ever lead to successful outcomes.

Here are some tips on how to resolve conflict:

1. Disassociate yourself from the conflict

You need to put yourself into the position of the observer. This is a place of no emotions. You need to watch yourself with the conflicting party. Take the emotions out of the conflict and you will get more wisdom. Put yourself into the emotions of another and handle the conflict.

2. Disassociate yourself from the person

How hard is it to negotiate when human life is at stake? When the stakes are high for other people, and there might not be a winning situation because of external factors and players but a good outcome is critical. Your feelings or wellbeing might be at stake when you are resolving the conflict for other people. Most people focus on negotiation when human life is an "object." This is so you can negotiate and save as many lives as possible. When preparing yourself for conflict resolution, take a tactical standpoint to help out.

3. Build rapport

We've covered this above but you have to remain calm. You must match the tonality, speed, and volume of the person you are in conflict with WITHOUT mimicking their angry comments.

4. Outcome frame

Having an outcome frame will help focus your thinking and you will be able to find an outcome. You will be able to succeed in resolving conflicts. In many cases, the parties like to cover old ground to lay blame. You need to ask yourself why you want to blame others. Will it get you closer to finding a resolution or the outcome you want? Create an approach that will solve your problem and use the skills you have learned to solve the conflict.

5. Listen actively

If we are completely honest with ourselves, we can all be better listeners. We only listen so we can respond. This means we often miss critical information that others are sharing. Our minds will naturally delete, generalize, and distort information. Remember that conflict is created from emotions and communication. Try to keep your focus on listening or trying to understand something from another.

6. Positive Intention

Many people who are in conflict will drown in details. Many times this is where the true argument stems from. On a high level, what does each part want security, space, love, or respect? Once you can identify this, it helps you create a better strategy to resolve the conflict.

7. Pattern interrupt

Many times during a conflict, it would be best to stop the chain of downward spiraling. This also interrupts the pattern. Make a calm statement such as: "It is important to me that we resolve our problems, but I need to take a moment. I'm going for a walk and will come back and resolve this problem in 20 minutes."

8. Step in somebody else's shoes

You've heard the old saying: "You can't understand somebody until you have walked a mile in their shoes." This still holds true today. Some people have a natural ability to be concerned with the needs of others. If you can put your awareness into somebody else's shoes, it could help you know what they are feeling. You could learn what they hear and see as you talk to them. It gives you an understanding of what they want and needs. Basically, it could help you understand them better. When you can take on the role of a detached person, you will be able to observe the interactions between others. This position encourages you to become impartial. You are basically watching the argument as if it were on the television. Watching the interactions between two people will bring a new perspective to the conflict. This new perspective will not be grounded in the views of either party.

NLP Applications

There are many aspects of your professional and personal life where you can use NLP. Let's look at a few:

Personal Life

Most people feel that there is something keeping them away from success. That "something" is often themselves. The best NLP application is getting control over your life.

Many people don't even know what they want out of life but NLP can change that. Once you find your purpose, it will help you align your values and goals. This covers family, relationships, health, career, and money. Being aligned can help you move toward success fast. It also helps you to get and remain motivated.

Most people hold only pessimistic and negative beliefs about their abilities and themselves. How you think about yourself will affect every single thing you try to do. It can either hinder or help your success. The main problem is many people think habitually.

You can also use NLP to reduce anxiety and stress. There are many powerful and simple techniques that many people have used to get rid of phobias and anxieties. There are other techniques that help you release unwanted behaviors and emotions from the past.

NLP is a powerful tool to improve communication. You can achieve this by developing rapport. This rapport can attract the right people to you. It can also be used to improve your relationships.

Business Life

Processes like leading and pacing can help improve sales. It also improves negotiation skills.

Having better communication skills could help you make stronger partnerships with suppliers, vendors, and customers. It can help you communicate with people who have different backgrounds easily.

These processes can help you understand and analyze the way your team members communicate. This help to create better functioning teams.

You will be a better facilitator and coach. You will have the ability to lead productive meetings. You will soon be the leader people want to look up to. The leader that people would love to follow.

NLP helps you will the hard parts of the business which is the people part.

Conclusion

Thank you for making it through to the end of NLP: The Ultimate Guide to Manipulation, let's hope it was informative and able to provide you with all of the tools you need to achieve your goals whatever they may be.

You've now learned many different NLP techniques. The next thing for you to do is to start using them. Practice makes perfect, and that's what you need to do with NLP. With some time and practice, you will be able to use NLP practices without thinking about it.

Lastly, if you enjoyed this book I ask that you please take the time to review it on Audible.com. Your honest feedback would be greatly appreciated.

Thank you.

Now, I would like to share with you a free sneak peek to another one of my books that I think you will really enjoy. The book is called "Mindfulness Meditation: A Practical Guide for Beginners" Published by Barrie Muesse Scott and Mark Davenport. It's an Introduction to Learn Meditation and Become Mindful Guided Meditation, Self Hypnosis, Subliminal Affirmations, Stress Relief & Relaxation.

Enjoy!

This book is all about using the power of your thoughts to be mindful and bring peace, purpose, and happiness to your life.

Drawing upon the rich tradition of Buddhism, mindfulness meditation is all about using your thoughts to be present in the moment and crafting the world that you want to live in. If you want to be more present in your daily life, this book is for you. If you want to heal and cope with chronic diseases, this book is for you. If you want to just sleep better or deal with your depression, then this book is definitely for you. Mindfulness meditation has been shown to have extraordinary effects on your life from your mental to physical health. This book will show you how to tap into the beautiful power of mindfulness meditation no matter if you are Buddhist or not.

The following chapters will discuss everything you need to know about embracing mindfulness meditation in your day-to-day life. However, an important distinction between mindfulness and meditation needs to be made before we proceed. Oftentimes, you see mindfulness and meditation used together. Other times, you may see mindfulness and meditations used interchangeably. Meditation is the more general term that refers to the practice of fine-tuning your mind through various mental exercises. Mindfulness is a form of meditation in which one focuses on being in the very moment compared to other types of meditation practices that may use chants or mantras. For the purposes of this book, it is important to note this distinction. Any meditation practice is great! However, this book will dwell on the importance of honing in on your breath with your mindfulness meditation practice.

Mindfulness Meditation: A Practical Guide For Beginners covers five chapters. In chapter 1, mindfulness meditation will be discussed thoroughly. How key concepts in mindfulness meditation relate to Buddhism, plus the benefits of mindfulness meditation, plus answers to frequently asked questions are included. The subject of chapter 2 is about how to practice mindfulness meditation. A practical guide about which positions are best and other best practices are highlighted. Chapter 3 explores more breathing and relaxation techniques that can be used to bolster your mindfulness meditation practice. The techniques in this chapter are able to help you vary your mindfulness meditation practice. Chapter 4 is dedicated to guided mindfulness meditation exercises that can help you as you begin your meditation practice. The scripts included will help you get started so you do not have to start your meditation practice from scratch. Chapter 5 is also dedicated to guided meditations, but the mindfulness meditation scripts in this chapter focus on guided meditations designed to heal various ailments.

This book about Mindfulness and Meditation will more than prepare you to begin your journey into mindfulness and meditation. There are a lot of famous people who practice mindfulness like Naomie Harris, Boris Johnson, Katy Perry, Richard Branson, and Anderson Cooper to name a few; thus, you are in great company.

There are plenty of books on this subject on the market, so thanks again for choosing this one! Every effort was made to ensure it is full of as much useful information as possible. Please enjoy!

Chapter 1: What is Mindfulness Meditation?

"To think in terms of either pessimism or optimism oversimplifies the truth. The problem is to see reality as it is." – Thích Nhất Hạnh

How many times have we been encouraged to see the cup half full instead of half-empty? Oftentimes in western society, the push to be optimistic and to think positive is drilled into us from a young age. However, if one is beginning to become more mindful, the transition to mindfulness may feel a little jarring as it is opposite of what feels comfortable. Imagine this. Instead of focusing just on the positive aspect of life, mindfulness encourages a realistic outlook on life that embraces the good and the bad, the positive and the negative and the neutral. And this is where our book begins, starting off by learning about this effective way of living that has been used successfully for centuries – mindfulness meditation.

Buddhist monks have been using the power of mindfulness for over 2, 500 years. Mindfulness is the act of allowing your brain to rest while observing the thoughts that come and go in your mind. Mindfulness meditation is different from actively thinking and using your creative mind. When you are being mindful, you focus on an object, scene or sound that is calm and then let your thoughts gently amble by in your mind. Being mindful is powerful because if you are always caught up into being busy and always thinking about your next step, mindfulness gives you a much-needed break and makes you reflect on your pattern of thoughts and actions. It is the exact opposite of the daily living experience of most people because instead of going, mindfulness encourages you to slow down the pace.

Mindfulness allows you to know your thoughts instead of trying to change them. Instead of being judgmental and unkind to yourself if you think something negative, mindfulness has no judgment value on your thoughts. Your thoughts are just there. When you are mindful, you are taking notes of your thoughts like a note-taker. When you are in a mindful state, you just pay attention to what your thoughts are doing but giving them the freedom to do what they want. Ultimately, the goal of mindfulness is to know your mind. Once you begin to know your mind, you can begin the next step which is to train your mind.

The beautiful thing about our minds is that they are malleable, and as a result, they are trainable. Our minds are able to change based on what one is thinking. If you think the world is a horrible place, you will operate from a place of fear and your actions will show that. If you think that the world is a wonderful place, you will operate from a place of reckless optimism without being able to be realistic about certain dangers you may find yourself in. Mindfulness helps you to know your thoughts and then begin to train your thoughts to become more in tune with your long-term goals. Mindfulness slows down the grind of your busy daily pace and gives you a different vantage point about patterns in your life. These patterns can be feelings that you have in certain situations or your reactions to how other people treat you. When you are being mindful, you may notice trends and patterns that you are constantly thinking. Are you always wanting more and more? Do you feel comfortable with the way things are? Whatever patterns you notice, mindfulness can help you pinpoint what types of things are causing you mental, anguish, conflict, or joy. Then after noticing these patterns, you can begin to shape it to how you would like to be by focusing on being more gracious, compassionate, and kind with your thoughts.

When you begin your practice, do not treat your mindfulness meditation practices as an obligatory item on your daily to-do list. When you meditate, you want to be present in the moment, not treating the practice as an aggressive measuring stick to how fast you can change or using your meditation practice as a form of escapism without being willing to change your ideals. The most important thing to remember before you begin is that you are training your mind to be at peace with how things are going in the world, no matter what is happening. Once you are able to be at peace in no matter what situation you find yourself in, then you are able to start to work on yourself to change your values. Mindfulness meditation is not a sprint; it is a marathon that you continually work on until you are finally able to free yourself from unsavory emotions that are clinging to you whether they are anger, agitation, negativity, self-image issues, unfair, hasty judgments, and biased opinions and ideals.

When you are training your mind to be more mindful, affirmations are great tools to use. Affirmations are very helpful, especially when you create them yourself. The thought process behind using affirmations is to use very direct language which influences your subconscious to help you get the outcome that you want to get. When you use affirmations, you want to first figure out what outcome it is that you want. Then create a short sentence with an active word. Make sure the sentence is in the present tense. For example, if you want to feel calmer and not be so anxiety-ridden, you can create an affirmation to help. You will start with the outcome of being calmer and make that into a statement using the present tense. Thus, the affirmation would be 'I am more calm.' By using the present tense, you are affirming the future outcome. When the affirmation is created, you can say it during your meditation time and throughout the day. When you couple this practice of saying affirmations with your mindfulness meditation session, they work doubly together to help you get the outcome that you want to get. For example, you hear the term think positive all the time. It is because positive thinking can help shape your future to where you have a positive future. However, if you think negative oftentimes a reality reflects your thoughts. Our thoughts influence our subconscious which in turn can determine our reality.

Mindfulness meditation helps you shape your reality by taking the time to know your mind. Once you know your mind, you will be able to train it and ultimately free it from negative, debilitating thinking. Every step works together. Before you begin your mindfulness meditation practice, know that it is not going to be easy. It will be a journey, but if you are dedicated, you will see a difference in your life.

The History of Mindfulness Meditation

For Buddhists, nurturing mindfulness is the ultimate path to enlightenment. The point of Buddhism is to reach the highest truth by focusing on overcoming the limitations that your body has. Buddhists practice mindfulness by using four foundational truths of mindfulness. The four truths originate from a Buddhist sutta or sutra which is similar to a form of Buddhist scripture. The name of the sutta is called "The Discourse on the Establishing of Mindfulness" or the *Satipatthana sutta*. Please remember that the four establishments of mindfulness come from a very long and rich history. This book cannot possibly cover everything related to them, but hopes to serve as a general overview that can deepen your understanding of mindfulness meditation. The four truths are mindfulness of the body, mindfulness of feelings, mindfulness of consciousness and mindfulness of phenomena. Each foundation normally goes step-by-step in a flowing manner. You can go in and out of meditating upon each truth. They all work together. The first stop on the mindfulness journey is mindfulness of the body.

What is the one thing that you typically hear before beginning any form of meditation? The answer is watching your breath. Most meditation practices or guided meditations instruct you to begin by taking deep breaths in and exhaling deep breaths. Therefore, when you practice mindfulness, the first step is to think about mindfulness of your body. Initially, you'll want to start by being mindful of your breathing. Notice how deep or how shorts your breaths are when you start your meditation session. There are also different forms of body mindfulness you can focus on as well, such as mindfulness of eating or mindfulness of how you walk. These are some of the easiest mindfulness of the body to begin with, but we will focus on mindfulness of breathing since breathing is key to healing lots of ailments, physical and mental in your body.

Mindfulness of the body is just not about the positions your body is sitting in or how you breathe, eat and walk. Mindfulness of the body also involves a deeper understanding of how all your body parts work together. This includes how your leg connects to your thigh, how your ears function, or the power of body working throughout your body. Mindfulness of the body also seeks to understand some of the more unpleasant bodily functions such as urine or snot boogers or blood. The purpose of being mindful of your body is to reflect on how your body functions. You may ask, how do I try to be mindful of my body when I am meditating? An easy introductory way to do this is to imagine yourself greeting and thanking each body part for what it does. You can start at your feet and work your way up until you reach the top of your body.

The next foundation you should be concerned with when practicing mindfulness meditation is mindfulness of your feelings. A better way to explain mindfulness of your feelings is that this truth is concerned about being mindful of your neutral, painful, and pleasurable feelings. You can also reflect on how to be mindful of these feelings by using the senses of your touch, smell, hearing, seeing, taste, and your mind. In Buddhism, your mind is considered a sixth sense. It important to be mindful of these feelings because when you have painful feelings they can lead to fear and hatred. Too many neutral feelings can cause you to become disinterested and floated through life. When you are neutral about something, you are not concerned about it and as a result, it will not be important to you. Lastly, you have to be mindful of pleasurable feelings because too many pleasurable feelings can lead to lust and greed. It is important to be non-judgmental and only observe your thoughts, not acknowledge them when you meditate. The reason you do not want to acknowledge anything is that once you begin to acknowledge a thought as a neutral, painful or pleasurable feeling, you are in danger of attaching yourself to feelings that will prevent you from being enlightened. Thus, it is best to use mindfulness to observe when you are gaining feelings of neutrality, pleasure or painful so you know how to handle those feelings appropriately. When you practice mindfulness of feelings, you will still experience feelings.

Mindfulness of feelings does not mean that you do not feel. It only means that you are able to enjoy the feelings without going overboard to the point of the feelings cause you to become obsessed and overly attached to the thing that is causing the feeling, whether those feelings are good or bad. For example, if you love doughnuts and you find yourself obsessing over doughnuts, you can enjoy them so much that you want more and more doughnuts because of the pleasurable feeling that doughnuts give you. Eating too many doughnuts can cause issues your health like diabetes or chronic inflammation. All of these feelings started because of the seemingly innocent, yet pleasurable feeling of liking doughnuts. On the other side, if you are leery of a certain political leaning and it brings you immense pleasure, attaching yourself to that displeasure can quickly lead to hatred and biased feelings. However, if you are able to know your thoughts and know that this political leaning causes displeasure, you can work to be mindful that the political leaning is a trigger for you without attaching too much to that feeling to the point that it goes overboard. Likewise, if you feel neutral about a person, you can become so disinterested in them that you lose focus of the fact that they are human and worthy of respect. Hence, if they ever needed something, you would most likely overlook them or drag your feet to help them. So even feelings of neutrality can be dangerous. Once you become too attached to any type of feeling, the excess doting on the feeling prevents you from reaching enlightenment.

The next foundation of mindfulness meditation that you want to build upon is mindfulness of your consciousness. In Buddhism, there are 52 mental formations. Mental formations translated loosely are emotions and states of mind. The mental formations are normally grouped together in a specific way. The first of these formations are the previous feelings that were discussed in the mindfulness of feelings consisting of feelings of pleasure, neutrality, and displeasure. The next 51 formations are what the mindfulness of the consciousness helps you to focus on that are clustered in different groups. These include:

- Proficiency of mental properties
- Pliancy of mental properties
- Perception
- Composure of mind
- Appreciation
- Effort
- Righteousness of mind
- Worry
- Desire to do
- Amity
- Psychic life
- Error
- Perplexity
- Feeling
- Right livelihood
- Volition
- Initial application
- Attention
- Greed
- Buoyancy of mental properties
- Adaptability of mind
- Recklessness
- Right speech
- Sloth
- Discretion
- Proficiency of mind
- Modesty
- Conceit
- Right action
- Faith
- Buoyancy of mind

- Pliancy of mind
- Contact
- Deciding
- Concentration of mind
- Torpor
- Mindfulness
- Disinterestedness
- Envy
- Shamelessness
- Adaptability of mental properties
- Distraction
- Composure of mental properties
- Dullness
- Balance of mind
- Sustained application
- Pity
- Selfishness
- Reason
- Righteousness of mental properties
- Hate

This is a general overview of the mental formations, but you can study them in more detail to get a more detailed understanding. To simplify this foundation, when you are practicing mindfulness of the conscience, be observant of the different feelings that go in and out of your brain. To easily start meditating with mindfulness of the conscience, when you meditate observe any thoughts that you have. When your mind drifts from focusing on your breathing, you can call out to yourself that you are being mindful. When your mind begins to drift from not meditating, you can call out to yourself that you are not being mindful. This simple exercise is using mindful of your consciousness. It is also a great trick to use in your everyday life when you want to be more mindful.

The last foundation of mindfulness that you want to build upon is mindfulness of phenomena or mindfulness of perception. When you think of a car, you know it is an object that has four wheels and has the capacity to take you here and there. The idea that you have in your mind of a car may be realistic and based on a car that you know personally. Or the idea of a car that you may have can be based on what your perception of what a car is generally, according to your knowledge of what a car is. When you practice mindfulness of mental objects, you try to focus on the 'why' of how you perceive something. If you think of cars as positive, this positive association could be because of a childhood memory that when growing up you had a wonderful experience of your parents taking you to school every day in an old beat up, yet comfortable car. If you have a negative perception of cars, it could be because your friend was killed by a car or cars cause you to think of all the damage that they do to the ozone layer. Mindfulness of perception allows you to focus on the experiences that shape your perception of what something is so you can bypass those perceptions to get to the true meaning of what something actually is and not what you think something is.

When you practice mindfulness of perception, you want to be aware of things that can cause your perception to be tainted. These can be known as the 5 hindrances. You also want to be mindful of the 7 factors of awakening which should be what you aspire your perceptions to be based on. When all of these factors work together, it helps you eliminate suffering. The 7 factors of awakening that you want to focus on when you practice mindfulness of perception include:

- Equanimity – This factor can be described as the calm observance of things around you.

- Energy – This is the energy that powers you to lead the investigation to seek understanding about different topics in life.
- Concentration – The complete focus of the mind is what this factor seeks.
- Investigation of your perception – This factor encourages you to seek knowledge about phenomena to understand how something operates.
- Joy -Balanced pleasurable interest in something is what this factor is all about.
- Tranquility – Serenity and quietness encompass this factor.
- Mindfulness – Present moment awareness describes this factor.

The 5 hindrances to avoid are:
- Dullness – Doing your takes half-heartedly with no vim or lacking concentration.
- Lust – A craving for pleasure to fulfill all your senses.
- Ill will – Feelings of hatred directed to others.
- Restlessness and worry – This is when you are unable to calm your mind.
- Doubt – A lack of trust or conviction.

When you monitor your thoughts to see if any of the 5 hindrances appear in your train of thoughts, you want to note when and why they arose. You'll also want to note how you can prevent the hindrance from appearing again and how you can replace the hindrance with one of the 7 factors of awakening in their wake.

As you work on your mindfulness meditation, strive to attain the four foundational truths in the order of mindfulness of body, mindfulness of feelings, mindfulness of consciousness, and mindfulness of perception. This is ideal. However, you can meditate upon all of the foundations in one setting as well. So, if you focus on more than one truth at a time, that is ok as well. To truly attain enlightenment, you must find a way to master them all.

Lastly, mindfulness meditation helps you cultivate awareness of the "three characteristics of experience." According to Buddhism, if you do not understand these three characteristics, then you are bound to be caught up into an endless cycle of suffering. The three characteristics you should be aware of are the traits of impermanence, or *anitya*, dissatisfaction, or *duhkha*, and egolessness, or *anatma*. Impermanence means that all conditioned things will change. There is a constant change that you must be aware of. The next trait of dissatisfaction means that there is pain and suffering and no satisfaction in an unenlightened state. *Anatma* means that one should strive to act without an ego. These three are another aspect of Buddhist underpinnings behind the mindfulness meditation practice. These are great to keep in the back up your mind when you are doing mindfulness meditation.

Hopefully, up until this point, the case for why you practice mindfulness has been made. In case you still are not convinced, let's try to convince you one more time. So why mindfulness? There are lots of different meditation practices you can choose from, but mindfulness meditation is a great way to begin for a few different reasons.

Mindfulness is awesome because it:
- Helps you not be judgmental – One of the major components of mindfulness is to not be judgmental of yourself and others. This gentleness towards yourself

improves your overall self-esteem. It also encourages self-compassion for yourself and for others.
- Easy and fast – There is no set time to do it. It is super easy to pick up on and relatively fast to do. Your sessions can be as long as they need to be or as short as they can be. If you have a busy schedule, you can meditate for 5 minutes or however long is best for you.
- Reduces stress instantly -Because the necessity of breathing is at the core of mindfulness meditation, deep breathing immediately reduces the stress you may be feeling as soon as you begin your mindfulness meditation session.
- Improves your wisdom – Mindfulness meditation improves your wisdom because you are able to figure out what makes you tick by noting and understanding the power of your thoughts. You also are able to be wise about other people, because this system meditation improves your observation skills such that you will be able to observe others and make connections about their behavior in ways that you have not been able to before.
- No set way to do it – For some people, the fact there is no set structure may be limiting to them, but it is a positive because there is not a right or wrong way to do it.
- Relaxing and calms your nerves – Just like reducing your stress instantly, mindfulness meditation also relaxes and calms your nerves due to the power of breathing.
- Observe yourself in the moment – Mindfulness meditation allows you to be in tune with your thoughts and actions so you are able to get into the 'zone' a lot easier than before.

- Easy to pick-up – Did I mention how easy mindfulness meditation is to pick up? Once you have one session, you will be able to do more rather easily.
- Doesn't have to depend on anyone else to do it – Mindfulness meditation is great to practice on your own. So you never have to worry about if the teacher is going to show up to class or not. This meditation style is self-guided so you can set your schedule according to your convenience.

Thank you, this preview is now over.

I hope you enjoyed this preview of my book The Power of Mindfulness: Clear Your Mind and Become Stress Free" by Frank Steven. Please make sure to check out the full book on Amazon.com

Thank you.

www.ingramcontent.com/pod-product-compliance
Lightning Source LLC
Chambersburg PA
CBHW030122100526
44591CB00009B/494